AF480680

Eternal Whispers

Songs Of The Soul

HARLEEN KAUR

ISBN
Paperback 979-8-89475-271-6
Hardcase 979-8-89475-951-7

To all the girls who dream to tell their stories.

Speak up, love.

The wind listens and

Cradles the whispers.

They will reach my ears.

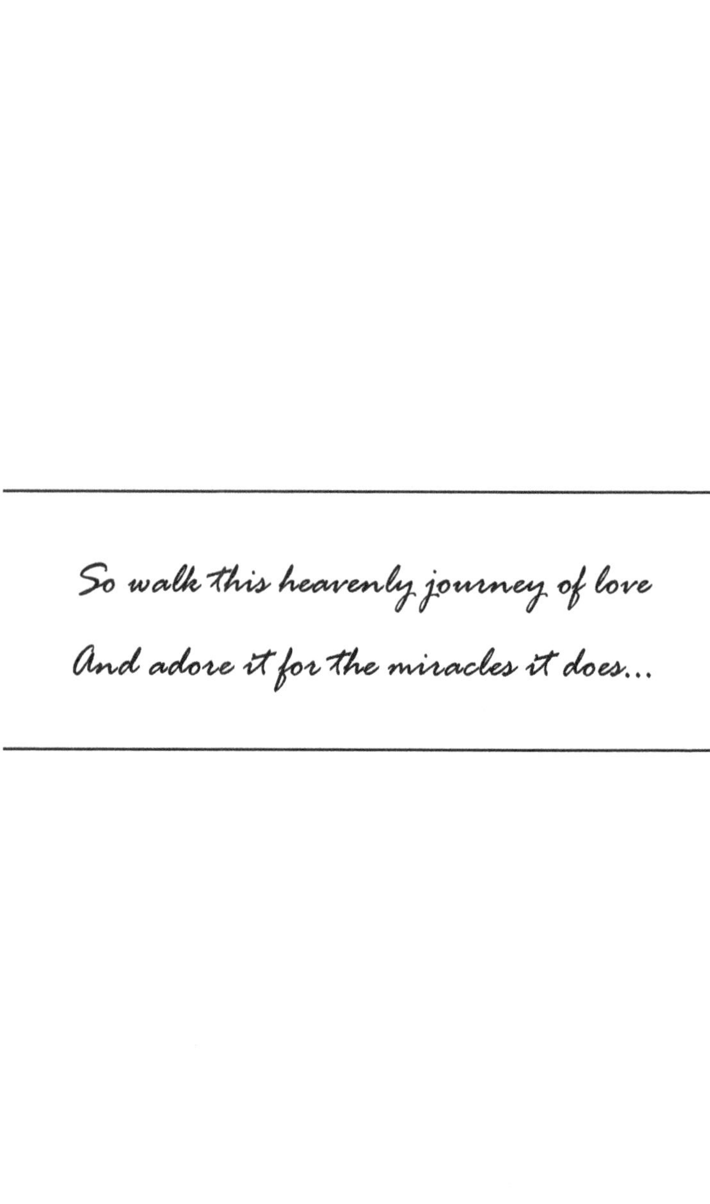

So walk this heavenly journey of love

And adore it for the miracles it does...

Author's Note

Hey there, awesome readers!

Welcome to my very first poetry collection, 'Eternal Whispers: Songs of the Soul.' I'm thrilled to share these poems with you. Each poem in this book is a piece of my heart, written during various moods and emotions. Some days, I felt like a hopeless romantic, and on others, a melancholic dreamer. This book is like a diary of my heart in verse form.

I've always loved telling stories through poetry. There's something magical about how words can dance and sing, creating vivid images and emotions that linger long after you've turned the page.

I often joke that my brain is a massive library with my heart as the librarian. So you can imagine the chaos and charm that goes on in there!

I'd love to hear from you! Feel free to connect with me via email at harleenkaurpoet@gmail.com or follow me on Instagram @harleen_kaur_poet. You can also find me on Facebook at https://bit.ly/harleenkaurpoet. Let's share our love for poetry and stories together.

To read the poems I used to write earlier, visit this website where they have been published! https://www.teenink.com/users/Harleen123

Thanks for joining me on this journey. Happy reading!

Cheers,

Harleen Kaur

Contents

Letters to My Tempest

Letters to my beautiful:

Thick, rough sheets, an ashen amber,

Fluttering against the azure skies,

Kindling love affairs like fiery ember.

Letters to my beloved:

The paper leaves are time-worn and crinkled,

Wrapped in envelopes, aged and venerable.

The frail, trembling hand holding it seems equally wrinkled.

Letters to my dearest:

Lush landscapes of adventures unfurled,

Letters bleeding longing in smudged scrawls,

Dry lips whisper the words, tenderly curled.

“Dearest Love,

I regret to inform you of my delayed visit,

The days here are barely passing,

Dark and hellish, ominous and rigid.

The war is glorified anguish

Like petals and thorns,

Everything seems frigid.

My eyes thirst for our lovely kids,

The many memories, I must miss.

Ava and Aaron, my little sweethearts

How long, I wonder, we have to stay apart.

Your thoughts plague me throughout the day,

I await nights, to meet you in dreams

Of saffron sunrises and moonlit veil.

Where intensity breeds passionate crimson cascades,

As scarlet silences and somber symphonies alternate.

I miss you, Aurora, your wicked tongue, your velvet voice,

The gleam in your alluring hazel eyes when you rejoice!

I miss you, Aurora, the feel of your hands,

The curl of your soft fingers in my palms.

I crave our long and crazy talks,

Autumn, pies and swings in parks.

I thirst for your loud laughs,

How they touch, my silly little heart!

I long for you, my wild, devilish tempest,

That evil tilt of your lips, enticing and luminous!

I will come home soon, my dear,

And hold you through the night,

As we watch stars dazzle in their velvet lair.

Ever yours, Edward"

Letters to my treasured:

Fingers trace the lines through worlds infinite,

Aphrodisiac to my parched soul,

Gulping them like a starved wanton,

Withering in their decline.

"My love,

Your words have become my elixir,

I hold onto those through fragile tendrils.

I am drenched in sweat of fervor,

This heartache feels cruel and unreal.

Wars are the paradox of mirrors and masks:

The reflective honesty in agony-filled wails

Is concealed under shadows of deceptive gales.

The whispers and roars of truth and lies

Can no longer penetrate the dusky haze.

Ava and Aaron are growing beautifully,

Like little flowers blooming in an enchanting mystery,

They miss you a lot, I myself crave desperately.

I believe we will meet soon, smiling. Hopefully.

Keep hope, dear,

You are saving so many mothers' tears.

I miss you, Ed, your sandalwood scent,

Your embrace makes me forget

Every scar and every regret.

I miss you, Ed, your sense of humor,

The secret winks, of a devious lover.

I miss you, Ed, your sweet dimples,

The way your seductive lips make me shiver.

I miss you, Ed, your emerald eyes,

The way they crinkle when you smile.

I will wait for you, love.

Just hold onto your heart,

Miles may separate us,

But heartstrings never part...

Eternally yours, Aurora"

Letters to my precious:

The sheets are damp, ink dilapidated,

Tears crust on the sheets in drops of crystal,

Why do my red eyes itch, still unabated?

Promises made and forgotten
Letters exchanged, now forlorn, sullen.
Waiting for decades at the threshold,
The whispering air has fallen cold.

One last letter, the woman reads
Her brain sizzles, her fingers twitch.

"To Aurora Kane,

We feel deep regret to inform you mam,
That Edward Kane has died in the battle.
His sacrifice will always be remembered,
Edward was a true and loyal patriot.

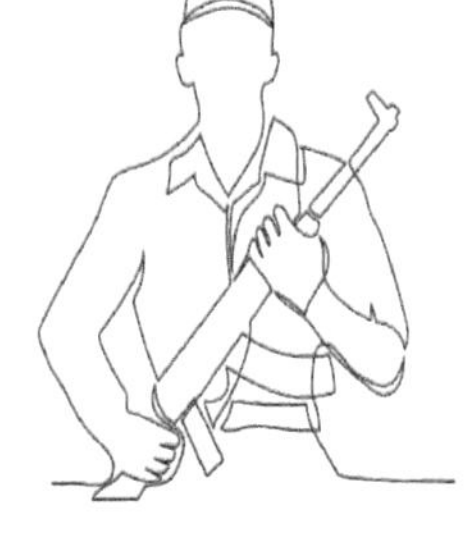

We, his comrades and friends,
Hope for God's blessings.
Please come to collect his belongings,
In office barracks, by tomorrow evening.

Unfortunately, a burial is not possible,
The body lies in the enemy fields.
The country mourns the loss,
His brave soul will forever be missed.
Commander Adam Smith."

Eyes closed, now silent and weak,

Moisture streaks dry on papery skin.

Head bowed and mind numbed

The heart beats twice, once, stops.

The boy became ash in the chars of war.

The girl died reading letters from before.

Hoping for a last kiss from her lover,

As the stars dazzled in their velvet lair.

In the air, however,

The scarlet symphonies still prance,

The old ashen sheets still dance,

Hearts fall silent and still

One dead and the other one killed,

But, as Aurora said, at last

The heartstrings will never part...

Auspicious Anni-verse-ary

Light up a candle, my dear.

Have a look, come here.

I wish to tell you a story of rush and dare,

Until the flames hush and fall bare.

"Oh! Do tell.

Is it a story about queens?

Swinging swords and bringing peace.

Or is it of that old wood cutter?

who brewed potions from salty tears."

No, little flair.

It's bigger than the fairytales,

Where the kings rise and villains fail.

It's beyond the panorama of old days.

A story new, yet timeless and vintage.

Their marriage!

It wasn't a cliché happily ever after of two love birds.

It wasn't a sweet fairytale with lovers aligning together.

It wasn't a ragged up version of falsettos promising forever.

No!

It was a majestic collision of the sun and the planets.

A vortex of colors splashing together

In a whirlpool of rainbow gauntlets.

Shards of cold blue ice against the red of raging fire,

Thick wild steam engulfed pleasure in divine desire.

"Did this explosion leave everything dormant?

Are the merry colors now dull and sodden?

Have the heart tremors subsided?

Has the floating glitter in the snow globe, landed?"

No, my love!

The hearts still prance with thrill and high,

High on the debauchery of sins and life.

Lost in the wonderland of virtues and vice,

On the cliffs of cosmic cataclysms,

Feeling breathless and alive.

"Then why they weep, on days' dark?

Tears falling like rough bark...

Why they lament the days, aghast?

How will this woven web of happiness last?

Are they fated to fail or cursed to fall?"

No, little dove...

Darkness is but a shadow's veil,

When light refuses to bow or pale.

Too much sunlight withers the soul.

Balance is the key, everyone should hold!

Light merely hides and resides under the cover.

Bidding its time, waiting for the charade to be over.

Love claims all, little lily!

The homes, again cackle with mirth and glee.

Being the men of earth, people commit heart crimes,

Succumbing to the temptations of shadows infinite.

But,

Do moons choose the planet they orbit?

Do planets choose their stars?

"The rules of fair play

Do not apply in love and wars"

Who are they to deny gravity

And laws of Leia, my dear?

When their love is brighter

Than any constellation in the star's lair!

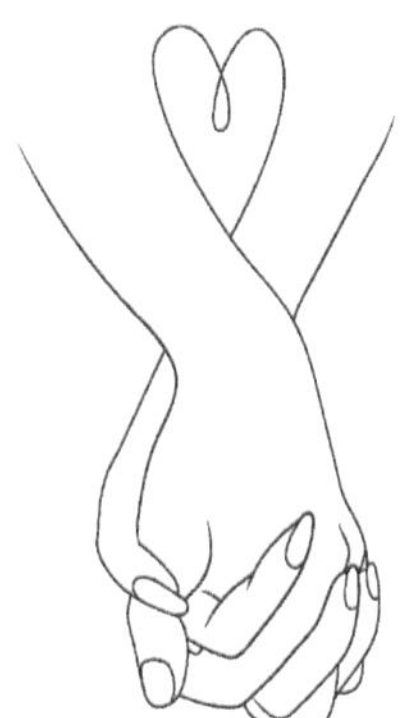

He claims their union indelible,

A souvenir, a treasure.

She claims it a blessed adventure.

Because, "What are games but opportunities

To either boast of victory or taste defeat?"

Marriage is a violent mistress,

Her beauty a mask to hide her cruelty.

The beauty of falsehood

Is the worldwide fantasy.

"Love is the irresistible desire

To be irresistibly desired."

It's dramatic like Giselle's ballet

And dangerous like Russian roulette.

So, when the life rears its head,

Showing teeth and claws

Those two souls smile slightly

And whisper, "Game on"

And then they wander the world,

Flowing in the winds of change.

Because, when together,

They forget how to breathe.

Apart, they realize,

"My other half has become my air, my need."

The Eternal Dance of Love

I am the ocean, wide and majestic.

Some fear me. Others worship,

The liquid is dark and deep and alive.

I listen to the whispers, even the quiet.

Beams of light, fall in a staged symphony,

Deep in my waves of crystal glass, so silently.

Water is a new trend in beauty and design,

Spilling bands of alternating colored light.

Delicate mosaics, floating as if on fire,

Waves of blue, silent in cold ire.

A whole kingdom of fins and tails resides.

The weight is heavy, of the infinite lives.

I don't ask, nor do I want anything now,

But sometimes I remember my old vow.

The way I begged to be loved and cared

The way I raged in tides, within its void

The way I tried to kiss the sky

Only to fall back in a shuddering cry.

It began with a drop, millennia ago,

My life evaporating to touch the cold.

I was hot all over, warm and searing,

My gasps of vapor escaped on winds.

My little kisses were caught by the sky;

He gathered them slowly, nearby.

I kept dancing in mindless euphoria,

Itching to jump and climb wearing talaria.

The enigmatic sky began to fill, falling hush;

Gray beauties of my essence floated lushly.

Cocoons of water puffs, like cotton candy,

In the soft embrace, grew glorious and heavy.

The sky couldn't hold the love anymore

He let it go, strings of shimmering gold rain

The water shone in the vibrant sun,

The drops fell screaming, itching to hold on.

I wrapped them up in my folds,

Howling in the agony it caused.

I wept and asked my generous lover

Why he couldn't keep me forever.

He bled tears of love, falling as rain

And asked me to trust him again.

Dizzy sparkling streaks adorn the artless sky;

He bellows in a deafening thunder play.

Eventually the dust settles on the streets,

Faint scent of humidity hangs in the air, replete.

My proposal and rejection for all to see;

I overflow with shame and humility.

Flooding the lands with my potent grief,

Trees adorn me with their green leaves.

And thus continues the doomed tale of our love,

Two silly ones playing, as heavens cackle above.

We keep reaching to meet each other,

As our love emerges in rainy feathers.

Sometimes I do get wrathful and livid,

Drenching the world in horrors vivid.

But sometimes I mourn softly,

Knowing love is the most costly.

Watching the tender blue cascades,

Like confetti for our wedding days.

Hearing melodies of star symphonies,

Dazzling grandeur of resplendent galaxies.

I sing gently the song of waves,

A tinkling laugh at my foolish ways.

Ah, the things we do in the name of love!

Tsunamis and floods-memories brim my trove.

Now silent and still, I reflect the sky's azure fame,

I have my pleasure, basking in fantasies of him.

Wings of Love's Flames

The shimmering, glass kingdom is dazzling,
Dotted with colored crystals that wink.
A kaleidoscope of rainbows alight
Bathed in clear waters and lush sunlight.

Glorious pools of emerald spill
Grand waterfalls, flawless cascades.
Aurelia stands beside the scintillating floats.
A blonde beauty in a rich indigo cloak.

Eyes glamoured in different hues
One hazel, and the other a brilliant blue.
Aurelia, the striking Glass Princess
Of the Kingdom of Radiance.

A bewitching land of majestic dragon shifters
Possessing flames hotter than the sun's core.
Iridescent scales shining like platinum silk
Jade crystal eyes, smooth as polished pearl.

Ruled by the just King Vaelen Skyblaze

Where children beam and peace reigns.

But safety is an illusion,

And lethal if forgotten.

Fate starves for misery like a glutton.

An ancient feud fueled by the neighboring Kingdom

Bitter venom piled up by ignorant rulers.

A war between "Emberlyn" and "Radiance" ignites

The nature weeps in furious thunders and cries.

Aurelia paces her chambers, uncertain and tense

Her somber mood, shared with a dear friend.

"The war has become more bloodthirsty

I fear our streets flooded with blood."

Nova gazed deep into her asymmetric eyes

Normally vibrant, were dimming as fear rose.

She had known Lia since they were little girls

Unaware, playing with their dragon fire.

"You are the princess, Lia

Have faith, let go of fear.

Protect your people with head held high

A Skyblaze never backs down or hides."

Aurelia loved Nova like her own sister

Filled with resolve, her mind now clear.

"Yes! Let's remember our ancestors of old

And follow their message that Love claims all"

Long before, when there was no opulent glass

And the land was adorned in moon forests dark.

'Ophelia' was the most revered and feared dragon

Molten gold eyes rimmed in exotic silver.

Hunted for her scales and magical wealth

Ophelia hid in fear of death.

King Cormac of Emberlyn was a greedy tyrant

He himself led the awful hunt.

While Cormac's son handled their kingdom

Ophelia was captured, shattering her freedom.

Mad King Cormac was filled with wicked glee

He underestimated Ophelia's thirst to be free.

A fierce duel erupted between Ophelia of 'Radiance'

And the Emberlyn King who reeked of violence.

Massive dragons blocking the sun,

Darkness overshadowed the city's every turn.

Burning cities and broken lives

Howling moans cleave the quiet.

Children orphaned, parents without child

Hope crushed savagely, leaving families half alive.

"Cormac must meet his end and die

My land can't handle any more goodbyes"

Ophelia's reptilian eyes blazed in red ire

She unleashed her lava-like thirsty fire.

King Cormac Silverclaw burnt to a crisp

Only ashes left, dark and unyielding.

The sky heavy with dark promises.

Pyres burning in agonizing embers.

Perils of war, gut wrenching and foul.

With a heavy heart and fractured soul,

Ophelia now ruled "Radiance"

As Cormac's son sought Vengeance.

This was the beginning of grudges

Hundreds of lives in battlefields.

Now, the bells have again started to ring

Aurelia's kingdom suffers brutally.

In the kingdom of "Emberlyn"

King Eldric Silverclaw and his son.

"This war is meaningless, father

Such horrendous death and destruction".

Prince Rowan wanted to end the bloodshed
"You are so disappointing, such a disgrace."
Rowan winced at his father's cruel words
His life marked by insulting shards.

"Why are we hung up on the deeds of the past?
How long will this unhinged insanity last?
We are opulent, fulfilled and rich
What else could you possibly need?"

"Your words are those of a foolish child.
My ancestors' revenge is now mine.
Those insolent 'Radiance' people
Deserve to die, turned to cinders."

King Eldric's face twisted in ugly hate
Rowan resolved to change this fate.
In the dead of night, as the blood moon shone.
He began the journey to Radiance, alone.

Through rough terrains, with utmost stealth

Amid lush greenery, he trudged ahead,

Passing glittering waterfalls of frothing water

Navigating deadly forests, he did not falter.

Aurelia and Nova training scores of people

In swords, crossbows and steely daggers.

A note arrived, unnamed

It was addressed to the princess.

Suspicions high amid tense ambience.

Aurelia read the letter in curious silence.

"Dear Aurelia,

I would wish you health,

But it would be useless.

Time is of essence

And I bring this message.

King Eldric's war is wrong

The stupidity has enough prolonged.

I miss the days of calm sunsets

When no smoke perfumed the air.

I have valuable information

Regarding king's battle formation.

Meet me tomorrow at first light

Where the blind seek magic sight.

I vow on my mother's honor

And my fire's purity and devotion

This meeting is not a trap

I just desire to help.

Your Well-wisher,

A peace lover"

Aurelia took her father's blessings

And went to the capital of "Skysing".

Accompanied by the royal guards

She reached the renowned blind statue.

There in black garbs, stood Prince Rowan

Aurelia blinked, surprised and shaken

"Well, this is unexpected"

"I would think so, your majesty"

Rowan made himself smile

To hide his poisonous dread rise.

"Did you send the letter?"

"Yes, I am the infamous peace lover."

The girl seemed enraged and a little scary

Rowan admired her courage and fierce beauty.

"Do you have a death wish prince?

I could easily get you captured and killed."

"You could", the prince was utterly calm

As if his life wasn't under immediate harm.

She moved gracefully fast and sleek

Like a predator towards a prey, weak.

A bloodstone dagger adorned the prince's throat
"Now speak before I make your soul float."
"What I said in my letter was true
I have knowledge to help you."

"Why would I believe the son of a tyrant?"
"Because I am here against my every instinct"
Aurelia inspected the prince silently
As if she could see every scar he held deeply.

He was dressed in black court finery
Yet his eyes were glowing fiercely.
His hair disheveled, dotted with stray leaves
He smelled like wet earth and floral crisp.

"You will accompany us to the court.
Try anything funny, and lose your head."
Her dagger nicked his skin, a lover's caress
Rowan found himself amused by the princess.

"I would behave myself

Even if you seem

Terribly obsessed

By my head"

Aurelia glared

Even as her lips twitched

The prince was charming,

She had to admit.

A room was arranged in a nearby tavern.

Smell of beer, sweat and cheap ale thick in the air.

Rowan told about weaponry and supplies.

His father's battle strategy and tactics.

He became their war adviser

Leading them to victory faster.

Aurelia admired his determination and wit

His ultimate sacrifice for the sake of peace.

Months passed in a brutal conflict

Death stained every city and district.

Emberlyn's backbone broken

Due to the prince's bold treason.

As the boy and the girl grew closer.

A blossom of love and tenderness amid horrors.

Eventually, a meeting was organized

As King Eldric wanted to surrender and apologize.

"What do you think about your father motives?"

"I don't believe him, he is arrogant and vile

He is planning something,

We must be vigilant during the meeting"

They clutched each other's hands

Entering the throne room with heads held high.

A cavernous hall boasting indoor waterfalls,

Large tapestries and wreaths of flowers.

Eldric glaring in betrayal at his son

King Vaelen, sitting at his ornate throne.

Nobles in resplendent attires all around.

Aurelia smiled as happiness abounded.

"I am proud of my daughter

And grateful for prince Rowan.

Let us join hands and pray to the lord

For a vibrant future and peaceful accor..."

His voice cut off, silent and sudden

Eldric's sword at his neck, gleaming

Rowan was quick with his own dagger.

Pointed lethally at his father.

"I won't let you end any more lives

Your meeting reeked of deception and lies.

Vengeance is a cheap reason to exist

Love is the reason this world persists"

Eldric was taken to the dungeons

While Aurelia stood in shocked gratitude.

A collective sigh of relief heaved.

Nova and the others grinned.

"I think a marriage is in order"

The king smiled at his daughter,

While she blushed a deep scarlet

As prince's eyes twinkled.

Rafflesias and sunflowers radiating joy

Under the sunset sky, tweeting birds enjoy.

The scent of gardenias and grandeur take flight.

Wide canopied trees scattering beams of light.

The skies again washed in pink and purple

Royal courtyard perfumed in cherries and maple.

Wisterias and willows glowing like fairy lights

Blissful bubbles of glitter dazzling bright.

Glass sculptures with enormous wings

Spilling patterns, alight with sun's kiss

An era of fresh cheerful dawns

In "Radiance" and "Emberlyn"

Aurelia adorned in a deep forest gown

Blazes of dragon fire alight in her crown.

Glowstones flickering in her hair

Unmatched eyes winking in a dare.

Rowan himself commanded a lush jade cloak

Eyes filled with tears of love and hope.

Aventurine crystals glistening in the sun

Cherry blossoms rain as festivities begin.

Together at last in each other's embrace

Sky covered in Wings of love's flames.

Red love amid dead blood, a hearty gift.

True serendipity as every sorrow uplifts.

Waves of Life and Love

The water sparkles like fractured glass,

As sharp beams of light partially pass.

The waves dance in the cool winds,

Fluttering up and down like enchanted wings.

The sun paints hot yellow lanes on the sea

As it twirls with a child's pure glee.

I inhale the fresh, saline air,

My heart and soul laid bare.

My lungs inflate like a water bubble,

Forming and popping like a cards castle.

My lips stretch into a wide, bright smile.

Reflecting in my brown curls and hazel eyes.

Felicia Dyer, a fierce marine biologist.

This year, I lead a new team.

I love exploring the unknown

And nature remains the greatest mystery.

I train and prepare the eager minds,

Sharing my passion with the young and bright.

I walk inside my grand seaside mansion.

Everything is ready to welcome my team.

Four people stand on my arrival,

Offering wide grins as if to rival.

I shake my head, slightly amused

Then begin our new pursuit.

"Warm morning to you all, here

I am Felicia Dyer, your new trainer.

Let's begin the introductions first

And then quench our knowledge thirst."

Nova and Aylin are twin sisters

While Zale and Kian appear like brothers.

We discuss, listen and debate together

My team is exceptionally skilled and better.

This year we have the 'Deepsters' program.

The winner is the one whose team

Learns about the suspected new species

Wandering through the undersea tides.

"You're such an awesome leader

I am sure, we'll be the winners."

"She's right, you're amazing

Felicia the facilitator has such a nice ring"

We all laugh in rainbow symphonies

The twins certainly know how to be funny.

They both have dew-kissed green eyes

Blond hair streaked with blue highlights.

"You are very knowledgeable, Felicia."

This comes from Zale,

His eyes, the palest blue, like sea and sand.

He smiles, bows and kisses my hand.

I blush rose-red like an ocean perch

He looks like the God Poseidon.

Kian elbows him as the twins giggle

"You all can leave now, enjoy your dinner."

My team departs in a flurry of noise.

I am left drowning in Zale's voice.

This year's 'Deepsters' challenge is daring

With 'Sperm Whales' to be studied.

We agree to go for an undersea dive.

I make arrangements for a submarine.

The mission is both dangerous and risky

We need to be overtly covert and stealthy.

The voyage is scheduled after two weeks

In the meantime, we all study and seek.

One fine day, as the dusk came

We decided to play a sand game.

The one who makes the best castle.

Will get whatever they wish.

The sky seems to drown in colors

Vivid brushstrokes of pink and purple.

Orange, yellow and red clouds

Seem to dab the overflow bowl.

While the ocean devours the hot sun

And wind demolishes the sand dunes.

Zale wins the castle making contest

His creation is detailed and artistic.

"Well, I worked so hard to impress

Felicia, don't you think I deserve a kiss?"

She pushes him playfully, and he laughs

His laugh, husky and deep, ignites her veins and heart.

As the sun sets beyond the horizon

They kiss like light touches waves in rain.

A soft inhale, a deep taste,

Careful touches as nature plays.

They sit in the cushion of sand, snuggling

As the melodies of water lower to whisperings.

And then the mission day arrives

Ocean gear and warm-up dives.

Nova, Aylin, Zale and Kian

All set for the grand leaping.

Down and down, we go deep into the sea

Observing the wildlife flourishing underneath.

Our submarine is connected above.

A team sits to supervise our path.

Long wisps of sea grass swing.

The coral reefs are simply dazzling.

We observe and take notes, lush.

Schools of fish pass by in glorious rush.

Sea dragons and jellyfish seem in a frenzy

Swimming with surprising ferocity.

I frown, concerned at the oddity

Zale plants a kiss on my palm, softly.

I smile and try to ignore the rushing fauna.

It's never easy. I should have known.

The submarine jolts violently

The controls spin wildly.

We tumble through the sea in disarray,

Like a stone bouncing down a mountain.

We hold on to each other, screaming

As windows blur and everything spins.

"I'm going to puke, get aside."

Nova heaves pitifully inside.

A rancid scent fills the small space

I plug my nose, fighting the nausea.

It seems we have lost our connection

We dive down at high acceleration.

A sudden stop pops my pressured ears

My hands shake, while wiping tears.

Aylin hugs an unconscious Nova,

Kian looks out and pales all over.

We had launched straight down

Crashing into a whale, huge and round.

It looks angry, agitated at the accident.

We screech like banshees at a rodent.

Aylin and I are leaking tears like taps

Zale and Kian look ready to collapse.

I try to contact the people above

Only to receive beeps in response.

"What do we do? You're the leader!"

Aylin asks, as her twin's pulse lowers.

We can't get out, not with the shark

We have no way to go to surface, back.

I am out of options, frantic and afraid.

"Calm down, Felicia. Breathe and think."

But the shark has lost its patience

It growls and throws us up and up.

We float as if in freefall.

Somersaulting, my heart stalls.

The beeping turns to a distorted voice,

"We're back on call.

Is everything okay?"

We shudder in heart-wrenching relief

Faces wet with sweat and grief.

We eventually emerge at the surface.

I see the sky, the sand, and rejoice.

All are given immediate medical care.

Such a bold life event we have shared.

Nova is awake by the next week
Everyone is better, although weak.
"We did it. We made it out alive.
Dance, friends. Let's celebrate life."
Zale is there with his calm approach.
I hug him tightly, deep and close.

In the end, we did learn about the whales
Although we endangered our lives in it.
We didn't win the 'Deepsters' challenge
But we thank the lord for our lives blessed.
The most beautiful thing about life
Is living through all agony and strife.

Afterwards, the five friends stand
Together, barefoot in the warm sand.
Singing glories of the untamed sea,
The wildness of nature's purity.
Holding each other's hands tight.
Watching waves shine bright.
Whirlpools of frothing water, white.
Enjoying the vibrant gift of life.
Scintillating serenade of flutes and fifes.

Dreamers Like Me

The day I first saw you, you were crying.

Fat tears cascading over your cheeks.

Broken pieces bleeding in sorrow's streaks.

Your grief seemed to overpower all else.

The unnatural depth of your feels,

I was amazed, honored to see.

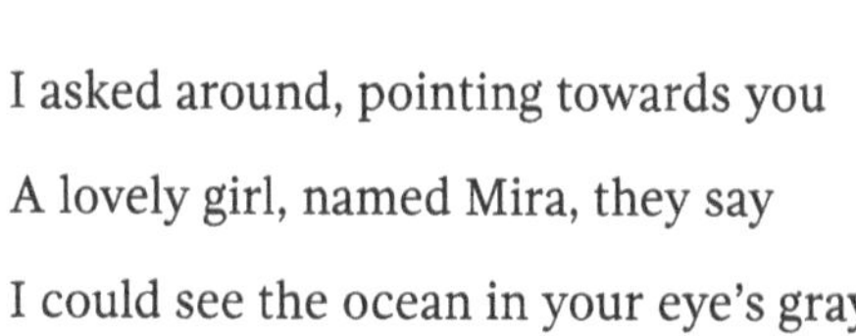

I asked around, pointing towards you

A lovely girl, named Mira, they say

I could see the ocean in your eye's gray.

A treasured wealth of emotions swirling there.

Wreaths of daisies and lavender whispering glee.

Wilted pools of hellebores weeping in agony.

I longed to speak with you.

To ask the cause of such misery

To sit and hold your hand, comforting gently.

Somehow, I steeled myself and approached you.

But you were no longer drowning, Mira.

You were lost in the dance of euphoria.

I was stunned, marveling at your pure ecstasy.

Who helped you climb up, dear?

What's the cause of such radiant cheer?

I stepped back, uncertain and afraid.

Someone came and kissed your forehead.

I watched you glow like water at sunset.

I withdrew, my heart slowing to a crawl.

I couldn't hold you through the night anymore.

Couldn't wipe your tears of bliss and woe.

Never knew if I could make you feel loved.

I'll never know the cause of your grief.

What makes your heart warm with relief.

But then I smile, laughing softly.

How could I think someone like me,

Could ever feel such passionate intensity?

These crimson cascades are expensive.

I don't even know their currency, dear.

How could I ever claim you Mira?

Foolish, I am such a silly dreamer.

Already making castles of tender hope, a future 'we'

I watch them sweep away in waves of your blue sea.

I sit back, close my eyes and dream.

Pink mornings in fairytale glitter

A hug from behind, a faint tremor.

They will help me live, while I wait.

That's the duty of dreamers like me

Creating utopian words of infinite beauty.

I chuckle to myself, then breakdown in sobs.

The hope of scarlet symphonies

Crumbling down to somber silences.

Heavens play the celestial waltz.

The sea could never meet the sky

A broken star is cursed to eventually die.

Cities crumble to rubble.

Clouds rain storms and thunders.

The only saving grace

Is in the pleasure

Of watching love, play.

So, I raise my eyes to you Mira.

You look like a goddess sitting above.

Ah! The ephemeral beauty of one-sided love.

Blooms of Doom

The hot air reeks of sweat and cheap ale

Chipped walls, painted in worn grays.

Hairs slicked behind ears, stiff with brine.

The tables are sticky with spilled wine

Courtesans scurry in salacious slips

Drunkards shout through loose lips.

Me and my friends sit around a table

In the corner of the over filled tavern.

'The Moonlit Mug' is far from alight

Dark in the desperate shadows of night.

I swallow back the muddy brown shot

It tastes like horse piss and doomrose rot.

Kethan's voice is grave for the first time ever.

"Two families got infected today, here."

My breath hitches at the awful reminder.

The plague was becoming a deadly killer.

Emberfall was already in tatters of decay

Our village seemed to be the next in its way.

People are dying like leaves in autumn
While authorities sit, silent and solemn.
Devoid of money, food and supplies
They starve, they sob, they die.
Hellbores seem to rain poison
Every person is snatched in its lair.

"The royals are just sitting slack in jewels
Where is the cure, or at least some help?"
Nyssa seemed to be yelling, her face flushed
"Insults have wings. We don't want you towed.
Don't drink, if it gets on your weak nerves."
Kyra shushes her sharp, while I observe.

Alden sighs, his teal eyes, dark, dull
Everyone seems lost in a ghastly lull.
"Don't be such weepy babies, guys
I am sure, we all will be fine."
Nevan's voice is slurred and heavy
Words dragging like hot honey.

"It's getting late, let's go home

Just pray and hope for good."

All eyes turn to me, as they nod

We all agree to meet next noon.

Alden helps Nevan to stand and depart

Kethan and his sister Kyra, tap their hearts.

I too, tap my chest thrice, as our tradition

One for strength, one for hope, one for elation.

I carry Nyssa back to her house

Laying her down on the meager couch.

I go down the black road to my lane

Where my mother awaits, surely in pain.

"Ma, I am back, how are you?"

Clogged breathing greets me, anew.

"Here, drink this tea, it helps with pain."

It does nothing, but hope is a saint.

She got infected just last night

I have told no one, due to fright.

The royal soldiers might isolate us

Then, we will perish in our own fuss.

"Have you eaten, Aylin, dear?"

Her voice has lost all its usual cheer.

"Yes ma. You just sleep and get better."

My lies are piling up like Nevan's beer.

I lay down on my damp, rough cot

Closing my eyes, in hunger, alone.

I have no money to comfort my ma

I am such a useless and silly daft.

My eyes weep like summer rain

Limbs quaking with dull pain.

The morning rushes in a burst of colors

Flowers blooming and grass in flutters.

The Sun and sky dazzle in gold and blue.

I glare at the radiant rays of white hues.

Why must nature dance in joy?

While my only family drowns in toil.

I will tell my friends about mom

They will help me. I am sure.

I reach the Temple of Aelara, iconic

The Goddess of health and healing, how ironic.

Everyone's present, coiled like a serpent

While health seems ominously absent.

I relate the news, sharp like a blade

Nyssa holds my hand, in silent help.

"I won't ask you all to risk your lives

I just wanted to inform you, guys."

"Are you insane? I always stand by you."

Everyone shrugs, as if to say, "me too."

My cheeks are wet like sponge,

Sucking a breath, I say, "Thank you all."

Nevan drapes an arm over my shoulder

"Oh dear, that's what friends are for."

We all laugh at his serious face

I tap my heart thrice, over the dress lace.

To healer Marcus's mansion, we stride

Our skin salty, heart chasms wide.

Guards halt us, standing tall like walls

I come forward, "Tell him his daughter calls."

As expected, Marcus comes running

He ushers us in, like potato sacks, hissing.

"Why have you come here, Aylin?

I left you behind, for a reason.

I have a new family and a wife

You are lucky, I spared your life."

I glare at the man, who is my father

He left us for his new life as a healer.

"I have no desire to dalish with scum,

I came here as the situation is grim.

Ma is struck by the plague

I need you to help her please."

His eyes widen, then narrow to slim leeches.

His forehead creases like crushed peaches.

"What will I gain by healing her?

I also don't have the required herbs."

I reign my temper, biting my cheeks

My friends seethe in similar hostility.

"A favor. Anytime, you may choose."

He smiles like a shark scenting blood.

A black stripe appears on my wrist, like a thorn

The mark of an oath, never forgotten.

"What do you need? I will get it."

"Pink doomrose petals are needed

Which grow in the 'shadow valley.'

The royals refused my request.

Buckle up daughter,

It's that hard to achieve."

Kyra scrunches her brows

"Aren't the doomrose gold?"

Marcus smirks that evil tilt of his

"Not the ones found in caves."

Nevan gasps while Alden pales

Even my heartbeat runs crazed.

The caves of shadow valley are death fairs

Large animals lost in bloodlust lurk there.

"I will get it. You swear on your life

To brew a cure and save my ma's life."

His wrist marked by a black stripe

We leave, our moods sour as lime.

"He is such a fetid and lousy ass."

Nyssa is back to her usual sass.

"Don't let that maggot get to you."

"She's right; let's focus and go."

Kethan says with a constant calm,

His confidence, cools my clammy palms.

A man arrives running, panting hard

His clothes look fancy; his head is bald.

"I am your guide, sent by Healer Marcus

I, Hamid, will take you to your caves."

We all gaze at each other, silent

Contemplating what this meant.

He joins us for our journey

We pack supplies for a week.

It's a two days' climb of grime and gore

I check on my ma, one last visit before.

"I will cure you ma. I promise."

I kiss her forehead, and leave.

Kyra stays back with my mother

"Thank you, you are a lifesaver."

She grins her warm, lovely smile

"I know dear, now go and pray to the divine."

Alden, Kethan, Nyssa and Nevan

Stand by me, as the route begins.

Kyra and I were once competitors

From rivals, we went to respect

Nyssa has been with me since age two

Nevan used to tease us all day through.

Kethan was our senior, the topper

We met Alden in the tavern, last year.

We stand by each other always

Whether it be gain or fail.

So, we tap our hearts thrice in unison

And begin the hunt for doomrose petals.

The breeze blows, whistling songs

While we walk the treacherous paths, long.

The foliage is thick, the flowers gleam

Clear water gushes in narrow streams.

Flocks of wooly sheep graze near

Misty sheets shroud the air.

Hamid guides us through trees tall

While mystic nature enthralls us all.

The twisted lanes are lined in wild ferns

The sun sinks into a foggy sea, alone.

The valley blooms red in dazzling grandeur

Kethan advises, a camp for night slumber.

Nestled deep into the roots, gnarled

We sit, we laugh, we talk, we retire.

The morning swings around in merry ways

I pray to Aelara, the goddess of grace.

"Guys, where is Alden? I don't see him."

I sit up from my bundle of banyan leaves.

Nyssa and Kethan search for his bag

While Nevan and I follow foot trails.

"Did you see him, Hamid?", I ask

He shakes his head, looking lost.

"Don't lie, or I'll slice you like a carrot."

Nyssa issues her threat with a dagger nick.

Hamid hisses as crimson drips down.

Nevan drags her back, calming down.

"Alden is wise. He will find the way.

We must move; time is slipping away."

I encourage my friend to climb ahead

While keeping a close eye on Hamid.

He takes us to a deep clearing

I start to shake; at what I see.

"I will tell you the way.

The rest is your game."

He leaves us, his bald head shining

As we stare at the skeletons lying.

The caves leer beyond the ivory shells

Their skulls grinning like maniacs.

Nyssa leaps over them like a butterfly

Running rashly where the caves lie.

"Well, it seems we have to go alone."

Nevan smirks, waving to the bones.

Kethan and I sigh, standing at the inlet.

We all stand together, peering inside it.

Darkness seems to leer, sneer, mocking

I shudder, tapping my heart, gawking.

I step my foot inside, just as the earth rocks.

My balance tips, and I fall down.

"Get down all!" I scream at my mates.

While sharp stones rain on like snakes.

"The entrance is barred." Nevan is dazed

Eyes wide, we all say, "What did we just do?"

Nyssa kicks a rock, "Damn that guide!"

Her speech is choked, face white.

Me and Nevan hold her hand

While Kethan just stares and stands.

Pinpricks of dull light scatter the cave

Only a few hours of sunlight are left.

We decide to go, wherever it leads.

To keep track, we drop seeds at our feet.

Moving though dirty puddles

We spot rotten animal carcasses.

The silence is breached by a low growl

We all freeze, as a huge creature prowls.

A serpent, dark as night

Howls, his golden eyes bright.

Nyssa and Kethan draw their daggers

While Nevan and I act as diversions.

"I am scared Aylin. Very much so

If I die, just remember, I love you all."

Nethan has no silly jokes to crack

We all truly seem screwed, at last.

Alden knew how to fight

He was our only bet in sight.

I leap onto its tail, thick with scales

Screeching, as it rattles and shakes.

Nyssa shoots a knife into its eyes

While it slithers like a ghost flies.

Nevan jumps onto its head,

I smile, thinking it will now be dead.

But the serpent is agile and strikes.

I smack into the wall, Nyssa cries.

Her arm gushes blood like a waterfall

While Nevan still hangs on its head tall.

While the serpent is busy in between us

Kethan lunges with a dagger into the guts.

It wails, a wretched wet gurgle

I hack off its tail, green blood puddles.

Nyssa leans on the wall, unconscious

Nevan picks her up, trembling.

I spot a shadow of a man

We all run into the cave end.

Stumbling, aching down to my muscles

Fearing for my lovely friend Nyssa.

Alden stands there with Hamid

Laughing, clapping and gesturing.

I breathe deep as scarlet rage festers

I pick up Nyssa's knife, as my heart curdles.

That damn man left us in the end.

I considered him my friend.

Nevan stumbles back, eyes wide

Alden has broken our might.

I see no point in hiding.

I step ahead, coming into their sight

Both men raise their hands on seeing us

Their jaws unhinged, brains shocked.

"Why?", I ask Alden, shaking with grief.

He shakes his head, "Leave me, please."

I slice through his leg like butter

While he weeps like street gutter.

"I just wanted some gold

Obviously, you all are so bold.

You came out alright."

He pants, heartbeats light.

"Nyssa is injured, you fool.

Now lie back and die in your own mess."

Hamid tries to run off

Kethan blocks his way, arms fold.

He stutters, "Marcus gave me money.

I have no beef with you, honey."

Nevan comes up behind,

And pushes that damn swine.

Guttural screams echo in the valley

As we stand, tired but alive.

I wipe my tears, Kethan stands grave

I see pink petals inside the cave.

Collecting the blooms of doomrose

We get down the path, trotting close

Alden hollers behind, swearing

Nevan carries Nyssa, weeping.

Lust burns, Love cuts.

But betrayal? It flays us alive.

We reach Marcus's mansion

Who acts joyous to see us.

"Where is Hamid, by the way?"

I smile, razor sharp as a blade

"Lounging down the Cliffside."

He pales, like sand at seaside.

He brews the cure, as sworn

The stripe vanishes like waning moon.

Nyssa's wounds are also healed.

"Did we win, Aylin?"

Kyra says, "Of course, dear."

We all laugh through our tears.

My mother looks better, her eyes so bright

"I promised you ma, I did cure you, right?"

Kethan consoles Nevan outside

Ma, Nyssa, Kyra and I sit beside.

Thanking goddess Aelara, eyes closed.

Gripping hands tight, sniffing our nose.

Together the five friends, stand in the light

Soaking up the lushness of dusk, alight

The birdsong warms the calm winds

At the edge of a cliff we all sit.

Gazing down at the crisp, clear fall

Mountains stand in the backdrop.

We tap our chests thrice, as our tradition

One for strength, one for hope, one for elation.

How the sun rises, erasing all gloom!

How death fell, by the blooms of doom!

Together we stand, hearts light and free,

Emberfall saved, by the friends' unity.

Our journey was harsh, fraught with fears,

But in the end, it bonded us dear.

Whispers in the Air

You stand frail in tattered clothes

Within the walls of a crumbling stall.

Your skin, rippled like water,

Your hands trembling with hunger.

Your gray eyes are dull and bare.

I hear hollow whispers in the air.

Gazing at you and your weak battles,

I pull a thing from my satchel.

A blank sheet, thick and yellow.

I inhale its musk, its inky mellow.

A pencil rests in my hands, unaware,

I hear inquisitive whispers in the air.

You move about, small and slow,

To help you walk, the winds blow.

Breads, pastries, and little cakes,

With soothing scents of luscious bakes.

You adjust the goods in your lair,

I hear delighted gasps in the air.

My calloused hands glide and whisper,

Sharp strokes and delicate curves on paper.

I draw the busy street, people strolling around,

As you wait, your eyes wide and round.

Their hopeful gleam dulls in despair,

I hear wistful wails in the air.

No one stops at your poor stand.

Its tarp is dirty, its colors bland.

Your offerings dazzle like precious gems,

Rubies, emeralds, succulent lems.

To make a living is a constant dare,

I hear the bereaved blues in the air.

My careful scribbles turn furious.

This cruel world, so empty, so spurious.

I wonder at the people's indifference,

I wonder at their haunting negligence.

Why are the laws of man so unfair?

I hear enraged mutterings in the air.

Your pink anticipation seems lost now,

Your hope drowns in the gutter, somehow.

Heartbroken, in hurt and fear,

You slump into your worn chair.

Even from afar, I see your tears.

I hear pitying moans in the air.

The pencil sketch is now complete.

A diamond of a girl in talent replete,

Stands out among the shadow fleet.

As people gawk, point, and repeat.

I come to you, smiling with care,

I hear enchanting stars in the air.

Your face blooms so beautifully,

A wide grin you give me, so graciously.

You try to stand on shaky limbs.

Your eyes scream with amethyst whims.

I ask for all the pastries you have here,

I hear rejoicing cries in the air.

You kiss the money I give, softly

I show you my sketch, silently.

You hug me close, just like a mother,

I close my eyes in love, so dear.

Your face is wet with hot tears.

I hear euphoric whispers in the air.

Your gray eyes dance in fiery ember

Burning like coals, yet so tender.

"I just lost my son. You're an angel.

I hope all your desires are fulfilled."

You kiss my forehead, ruffle my hair,

I hear joyous melodies in the air.

Later, I walk through desolate lanes

Gazing at clouds, as soft rain begins.

The tumbling drops land on me.

I think about your lovely treats,

Your sweet face, and close my eyes,

Soaking up the magic of nature's affairs,

I hear relieved sighs in the magical air.

Love Lanes and Candied Rains

The trees are alive with birdsong and winds.

Dandelion seeds floating like angel wings.

The sweet scent of cherry blossoms perfumes the air.

The sky above is an endless fairy-tale blue, calm and clear.

I saw him sitting that day

All poised manners and grace.

Looking larger than life

I was hostage from the first sight.

Eyes the color of deepest ocean blue

A sharp contrast to my warm hazel hues.

The man was alluring and addictive

Like fine wine.

Sending sensual shivers of lava

Down my spine.

He was sitting with his friends

His laughter rang like holy bells.

I was lurking nearby, overworked in a fuss

Running late or stressed, I guess.

The reason for my presence is forgotten

Like smoke lost in a cloud of sweet cotton.

"What remains etched in the memory?",

"This meeting", another of fate's cupid mysteries

I walk, no, I strut towards the enigmatic man

Or perhaps glide, floating on magical sand.

Our eyes lock, and electric sizzles, blaze

Suspended in a time lapse, everything else fades.

"Hello to you", the flustered man stutters

"Hi yourself", I murmur, as my heart races.

He gets up in an awkward tumble of limbs

Running a hand through his tousled hair, he grins.

The surroundings blurry and blush

His adoring gaze makes me flush.

My small hand engulfed in his

Deliciously calloused and sun kissed.

"What can I call you, gorgeous?"

"For starters, how about Goddess?"

"And your first name, goddess dear"

"I'm Olivia, known for my dramatic flair"

Chuckles and laughs, gasps and dares

Blooming pink glitter in the tinkling air.

"And who would you be handsome?"

"Guess?", And the girl hums.

"James Lockwood, at your service, my lady!"

He gives a theatrical bow, winking charmingly.

"Oh, what a charmer you are Mr. Lockwood"

She pretends to mock, as they talk late into the night.

From dance and music, to movies and culture.

Ugly pasts and picturesque presents, enrapture.

Souls dig each other down to the marrow,

Their lust to know, takes wings and grows.

Every butterfly in the world

Has migrated to my stomach

"James, you are in the air I breathe

And the blood in my veins."

"Your touch stays on my skin,

Your thoughts on my mind."

"How can this feel so

Achingly sweet and divine."

"Let me in.

Let me take care of you.

Give me your trust,

and I'll give you the world."

She was his wildfire

Untamed, his every desire.

He basked in the sunshine of her smile

Raining Asters to make her "forever mine".

Burning in rain's embrace,

Each drop is a kiss from heavenly fate.

In mystic hues of nature,

Hearts dance and flutter.

Honeysuckle's melody

Is sweeter than any love letter.

Blink and the weeks fall away like leaves

The bond deepens, the rainbow sky preens.

But calm indicates a bitter impending deluge

The tragedy strikes, horrendous and huge.

Ashen gray sky blending with a ghostly pallor

Whispers of decay weave through the air.

Olivia's parents crash into James' brother

The car accident renders everything to cinders.

Love is expensive.

Its currency is grief.

And sometimes, it costs

more than we can afford.

My mother loses her short term memory to amnesia.

James' brother is in a coma,

Fighting for his life, a treasure.

Love and loss are like majestic ships at sea.

The more we love,

The more we have to grieve.

The world feels,

A grainy blur

Sharp, yet sick and sore.

Tears are the language of grief.

And grief is the language of love.

It's fragile, like a wounded dove.

My mind runs

Unhinged and crazed

Like a lunatic beast caged.

My heart falls,

Listless, still and dumb

Like sand, chafed and mum.

It aches scorching

Blazes of ember,

Eating me up leisurely.

My arms are flailing

Like a little bird,

Falling head up.

The world is spinning

Twisting in static,

Chillingly haunting.

It seems

Like a movie

Gone wrong.

I beg, I scream, I flounder

I wail in wretched anger

I choke and I drown.

Photos are like exquisite fantasy fiction,

A convincing bunch of charming illusions.

But life isn't pics and shots, it's fluid

Blink, and it leaps forward, intrepid.

Ah! The solemn song of waves

Tranquil, quiet and rare

Beckoning me to a dare.

Calling me names

Hounding me ahead

"A challenge", they say.

Our devotion and trust is tested
Sleepless nights, hearts mutilated.
We hold on, hoping against hope
Tears hanging like death's rope.

I float in the cold
Embraced in a cocoon
Free and underwater.

Life is hard enough
without making lovers
of our demons.

But hope arrives in a halo of radiant yellow and golden
Confetti rains, as James' brother revives,
Healthy but shaken.
Olivia and James kiss in heart shaking relief,
Wrapped in a desperate embrace
At the end of potent grief.

My heart swells, like a flower in the sun.

The fate has had its sadistic fun.

Gladiolus and daisies bloom and rejoice,

I laugh unhinged, even as my cheeks are moist.

"It's over", I whisper shakily

"We did it, honey!"

The air seems to shimmer

As elation overpowers every fear.

"I love you James. With you, I hope to dare.

Your heart is safe; I will always protect it dear."

"Oh my love, my heart is yours."

He hugs her tight, never to let go.

Wisterias and willows, camellias and ferns

Seem to litter the garden of life's twisted turns.

"But we have walked the luscious love lanes,

And I can't wait to relish the candied rains!"

The World He Dreamed

He howls like a spirit possessed

Dripping blood veils his vision.

He stumbles, teetering on the edge of a cliff,

The enemy keeps on firing.

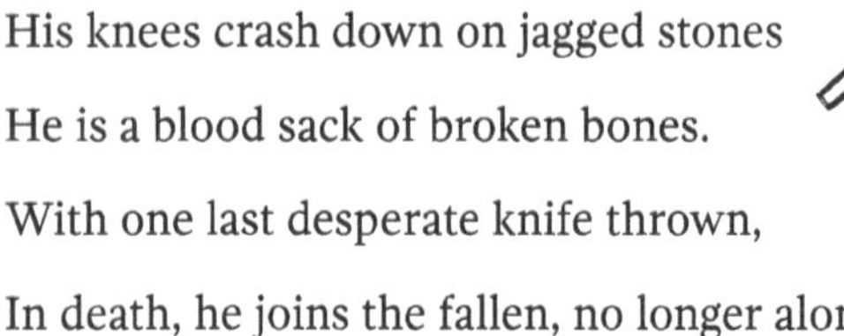

His knees crash down on jagged stones

He is a blood sack of broken bones.

With one last desperate knife thrown,

In death, he joins the fallen, no longer alone.

Memories flow in a scintillating rush

A lovely girl kisses his cheeks.

An old man gently pats his back.

His mother weeps proud tears.

Oh! The sensation is too much to bear!

Both men fall, an anticlimactic end.

They dream of wonders in their death.

Unknowing, he killed without a name,

Never knowing the names of the blood he spilled.

Is this how he chose to leave?

Alone within walls, his wife grieves.

He dreamed of a sky dazzling bright,

Gold and blue with silver stars taking flight.

Did he find the utopia he sought?

Or the land still decays and rot?

Was his death a cause in vain?

Blue pains and no gains?

Didn't once did he take a pause?

To ask if wars ever have a worthy cause?

Is this the world, he died for?

Where eyes are forever narrowed.

In disgust or judging,

In ridicule and sneering.

Is this the world, he died for?

Where the one in the scars of battle,

Must wears full sleeves in public.

Is the truth that hard to see?

Is this the world, he died for?

Where beauty equates to pain,

Name of the gullible game,

Played for fallible fame.

Is this the world, he died for?

Where a female soldier is ignored,

Her courage considered chaos.

Her survival seen as weakness?

Her broken nose, a sign of ugliness?

Is this the world, he died for?

Where one who lost his leg,

Is mocked as disabled,

Left to shiver as he bled.

Is this the world, he died for?

Where the kids orphaned,

Roam in rags, torn slippers.

Along the blood soaked fur,

Of filthy wounded animals.

Is this the world, he died for?

A torn shoe lies on the torn road.

A diary, half burnt in the flaming trenches.

A family photo, marred by dirty boots.

Is this the world, he died for?

A pink bag, full of crazy sketches

Gifted as a luck charm,

To make her father happy.

Is now the haven of the mice army.

Is this the world, he died for?

A baby girl cries for her fallen father.

The mother cradles her and the horrors.

A boy screams for his brave big brother,

A numb girl at the window, awaits her sister.

Is this the world, he died for?

The soil once fertile,

In fields of golden mustard,

Is left rotten and curdled.

Is this the world, he died for?

Ashes wet and swept in blood

Flies hover near the hollow corpse.

A broken arm is dragged away,

To bury or maybe burn in hay.

Is this the world, he died for?

Losing his comrade to infection,

The government can't give medication.

The rich, wipe their noses with notes,

While soldiers die like dominoes fall.

Is this the world, he died for?

Where people snort drugs,

Like bliss from God's nectar.

Perished bodies in clogged drains,

Black water, black nights and black lanes.

Is this the world, he died for?

Where there exists a cost for life,

Or should I say, a cost for flesh alive.

People plundered like honeybee's honey

Red tears, red blood and red money.

Is this the world, he died for?

Where greed overpowers the beauty of love,

Where power is craved like an addict on loose.

Where selfishness breeds like rats, unhinged

Where insanity and madness are unnamed sins.

Is the world, he died for?

Are the hearts not dirty anymore?

Has the poison bled for good?

Or does it still fester like rot?

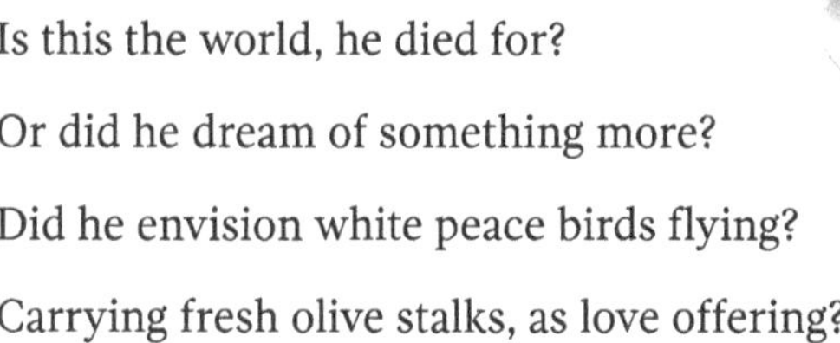

Is this the world, he died for?

Or did he dream of something more?

Did he envision white peace birds flying?

Carrying fresh olive stalks, as love offering?

Oh yes! The boy was a dreamer.

He thought love could exist

Anywhere and everywhere.

Well, it could exist. Couldn't it?

If we keep quiet and listen.

Listen to the melody of dancing petals,

The stories and legends of the old and weary.

Listen the fall of ice on trees, in parks

Listen the hoots of owl from afar.

Listen the scintillating serenades of stars.

Listen to the mellow of millions of flowers.

Listen, residents of this wonderful world,

Listen the nature and learn its hopeful accord.

The boy didn't die for the pity of the naïve.

The girl didn't suffer for your weak cries.

Love is forever, alive in smiles, I promise.

Sacrifice is forever, alive in pleas, I promise.

And you will feed it flames, I hope you promise.

My Thunderbird

Sandhya means the hour of dusk.

When the sky is vividly painted

In rich hues of orange musk,

Strokes of ochre

And serene pink blues.

My mother is a modern art.

An interwoven patch up of

Concealed truths and a prickled heart.

A perfect blend

Of vice and merit,

Of an overgrown hassle

And full fledge planning.

A high crescendo

Of frost melting glare.

Blazing tempers and

Superfluous virtue flair.

She craves truth and lusts honesty.

Drunk on faith and addicted to loyalty.

Rhapsodic to her core and hates blasphemy.

Cheese to my Margherita,

Chocolate to my s'mores.

Cherry on top of my pudding,

Calm to my soul.

She says, "World is too cruel,

It evinces, betrays and slays.

There is survival of the fittest,

And you must adapt to be your best"

She believes in inner beauty,

For her appearances are transitory.

Plants and greenery are her aesthetics.

Music and songs her amateur antics.

Pious to a high degree,

Sacrilegious and God fearing.

For her "To err is human,

And too repeat that error

is a sure crime."

Assumptions are her weakness.

An over-enthusiast tongue, a looped sling.

Unwrapped anger and unmatched pride,

Her pushing for frequent mental suicide.

But as it is often believed,

Idealism is too cliché,

Perfection is often bleached.

Allurity is rarely found in crowds.

It's, perverse and dark

Decorated with virtue shards.

Some honed to fatal instincts

Some blunt with subtle merits

Some sharp enough to shatter claims

Some smooth enough to pass as innate.

My mother is such an allurance,

A test of your worldly endurance.

A multitude of rarity in its ordinary own.

She is a diamond that doesn't refracts but shones.

They say, mothers end all bane.

I say, my mother is an all cure medicament.

They say, mothers bleed red for their child.

I say, my mother's veins flow with God's ichor.

They say, mothers are godsend.

I say, my mother is herself God incarnate.

These mere strings of alphabet

Don't offer her justice.

The epistemology of her,

shall never end.

Infinite as my mother is,

Her wildfire beauty

is far beyond me to comprehend.

Sandhya is not just another person,

She is the souvenir every one desires.

A multi-genre one-off novel,

Evoking fumes of unmatched passion and ire.

She is my brandy, whiskey, rum and ale,

Her personality is equal parts jovial, seraphic and morally gray.

I hate hugs, but hers is the one I cherish every day.

And I wish you today mom, a very happy birthday.

<h1 style="text-align:center">Paper Boats</h1>

You were crying that day,

Tears painting your hands

Like wet clay.

My eyes burned,

Watching you this way.

I just wanted

To ease your fears.

I was little then,

Maybe around seven?

You saw me and called, "Raven."

I hesitated but came,

"I want a hug," you whispered,

In pain.

A simple request,

from someone named Rose

I froze,

Afraid yet intrigued,

You stood waiting,

Your arms I filled.

"Why hug me?" I asked,

"You looked sad," you said simply.

And you looked like,

You wanted to help.

We met again, day after day,

You talked, I listened.

We made paper boats,

Huddled together,

In our little coats.

We grew up as friends,

Bound by invisible threads.

We laughed in pain,

Like leaves in rain,

We cried through smiles,

On silent lanes.

our hearts beat in sync,

like leaves trembling in blaze

I blinked, time leaped.

When life became hard,

We still made paper boats,

hopes folded into each crease

Kept our spirits floating.

It was your birthday, I remember,

I worked hard to earn.

Saved money,

Bought expensive linen.

crafted a swan with trembling hands,

a gift wrapped in love and effort

I was often cast aside,

But you shone popular and bright.

You had a party, I wasn't invited,

The irony cut deep,

A wound I couldn't hide.

I borrowed a cheap coat,

tried to blend in, impress,

brought a red rose,

As your namesake,

I suppose.

Your eyes met mine,

And turned cold,

A stranger's gaze in familiar eyes.

I stood there, terrified,

of this new, unrecognizable Rose.

"I didn't invite you," you hissed,

Like a serpent,

Spitting venom,

Shedding false skin.

I again stood frozen,

Silent and dazed,

My heart heavy,

My spirit crazed.

"But ... I'm your friend," I whispered,

My voice a fragile thread.

"Yes, but you're weird," you sneered,

"Go back, I don't want you here."

You laughed with others,

Waving hands.

Eyes, frozen islands

Of ash and dirt.

Whispers passed,

Insults hurled,

My soul crushed,

My spirit curled.

I saw you fake feelings,

I watched as you acted,

Felt like a fool,

realizing too late,

I was never more than a tool.

As if I could ever be like you.

I felt tears fall,

Surprised to see,

That I was weeping, at being free.

You finally made me taste tears, darling,

My heart broken, my spirit swirling.

I placed the rose and the swan,

Amid clovers and columbine in a vase.

You should have held an outdoor party,

But you never did appreciate nature's beauty.

Pink wreaths of dazzling flowers,

Clematis and candytufts, planted together.

I saw them there and laughed,

Poverty and indifference, oh, the craft.

The sky shone a brilliant azure,

Blushing in purple, golden hues.

I spotted a concealed weeping willow,

Sat down and breathed the moist air.

I pulled a paper out of my pocket,

Folded with care, each crease tight.

Now I make these boats alone,

No more Raven,

No more Rose

Thinking, I could impress

As if it made any difference.

The fragility of paper like life,

How quaint. How strange...

<h1 style="text-align:center">The Best Gift</h1>

"Who broke your heart?",

The Little girl asked the sky.

Wide eyes, innocent face,

"Why are you weeping a thundering cry?"

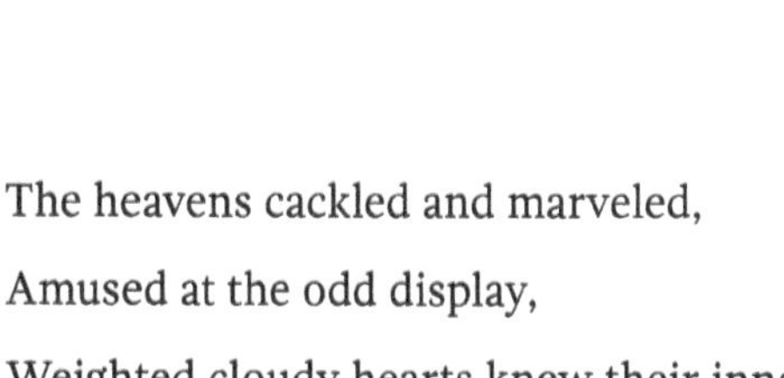

The heavens cackled and marveled,

Amused at the odd display,

Weighted cloudy hearts knew their inner ache

Never had anyone cared to ask anyway.

Girl's green eyes glimmered

Like dew kissed leaves in icy winter.

"Take my lucky leaf, it will make you happy."

Blushing, the girl held up a Rosemary.

The gray beauties thundered, laughing

Wondering if she knew

That it was the best gift

Delicate, heartfelt and true.

The Song of Universe

I want to disintegrate,

Disappear or just break up

into thousands of particles.

Like rain, I want to land on earth

wearing no parachute.

Just the cushion of wind and

Telltale of my own adventures as strings.

I want to live in clouds.

In the beautiful and calming abode

of hazy cotton lands.

To rest and sleep and melt

in the softness.

I want to fly, to soar and bank

and glide throughout the infinite sky.

To overcome with giddiness

and to live life to the fullest.

I want to cherish, preserve and make out the most

of each moment in my life.

To relish and revel in all the beauty gems,

scattered in my sorry excuse of life.

I just want to sing and dance.

To lose myself

In the infinitesimal song of the universe.

While shivering in the phantom winds,

Growing content in its debauchery and sin.

The Song of the Stars

The 'Shadow Kiss', sparkles with bliss.

Two stars draw close in a kiss,

Three stars encircle, adding to the mix.

A legend, from centuries before,

A constellation's forgotten lore.

Let's whisper the songs of the stars

And see what we learn from the past

Long before,

When the birds sang melodic lullabies,

And the winds played among trees, alive.

When apples and sugar perfumed the air,

And nature danced in a carefree flair.

A girl with rosy cheeks and a wide grin

Lived in the city of elves, 'Everglean'.

Unruly chestnut curls and golden eyes,

Glowing like ember in the pearl moonlight.

Akira, a conjurer of dark shadows and mist,

The most notorious in the wanted list.

An escaped fugitive, on the run to save her life.

Will she ever be safe from agony and strife?

"The daughter of shadows

shall bring the change.

Capture the dark wings,

Don't let them take wind.

When darkness is raised,

Hunt the gold framed."

Heir to the prophecy of the ancients,

Who warned of a golden-eyed deviant.

Banned, exiled, forsaken and left by her own,

An innocent child, pushed to shiver alone.

Forgotten facts often turn to rumors.

Assumptions are the death of truth.

So, I ran, through plains and forests wild.

To avoid execution by the cliffside.

I wandered for food, one dark night.

Spotted a camp, hidden from sight.

But, how can shadows fool their master?

I am their solace, their sole conqueror.

Four people appear, only one a girl.

Laughing, as firelight gleams like a pearl

They dance around and sing old songs.

I wonder how it feels to belong.

I shake my head and find their horses

I plan to steal a little food from saddles.

I call on the shadows, they cloak me

I steal, even though I feel guilty.

And just when I'm about to leave.

A hand covers my mouth, stopping me.

I squeal, struggling to be free

The man grunts, as I try to see.

"And who do we have here?"

A hot whisper in my cold ears

I stamp on the booted feet,

The man chuckles, dark and deep.

"Stop it. I don't want to hurt you.

Be quiet or I will be tempted to."

I still, panting like a dog,

Then I let the shadows dissolve.

The man grips my wrists, turns me.

My heart stalls, when I look up to see.

He looks like a personified carving

Glass blue eyes, deep and striking.

"Who are you to think you can steal?

Don't you have any shame, thief?"

One eyebrow arches in question,

I turn away in regret and humiliation.

"Interesting", he says as others arrive,

Who look at me, as if I am a dead rat alive.

To calm myself, I count till nine.

The girl says, "Hey, are you fine?"

"I... yes, I am,", I lied.

The girl lifted my chin

"I am Naia, what is your name?"

"Aza.", I gave a fake name.

Naia took me to their campsite,

Where she served a wholesome meal.

Others sat and observed

While Naia made introductions.

"The one who caught you, is my twin brother

Ezekiel. Others are Zayn and Asher."

She smiled, a kind and angelic one

A shock to me, after being shunned.

"I apologize for my behavior.

I was just caught off-guard earlier."

Ezekiel raked a hand through his hair

His arms flexing, eyes glinting like starlit air.

I travelled with them, to distant shores

Forming friendships, while doing chores.

Asher and Naia were a sweet couple

Zayn was the funniest person ever.

Ezekiel was lovely and stern all the same.

We talked a lot, playing the flirting game.

But I didn't know why they left their home city

They held their secrets and I held mine.

They thought I was 'unblessed'

Meaning, I had no ability to possess.

"Your parents abandoned you, so tragic!

Just because you had no magic?"

"Yes, I have been alone ever since.

But now I have you.", I grinned.

Naia and Aza became close friends

But still, a lot they withheld.

While Ezekiel and Aza grew closer

Like dew and leaves in winter.

"You are so strong and brave.

I still remember the day we met.

Awful beginnings are such a farce,

What matters is what happens at last."

His words lit me up like wildlife.

I preserved them while dreading future ire.

"You are such a charmer, dear.

Acting all angry and mighty like a bear

But actually you are an awesome cuddler,

A baby really, under that tough exterior."

I laughed at his affronted face.

He chased me in fairy lanes.

Naia and Asher had a beautiful bond

Like that of a warm nest and a bird.

Bubbles of bliss, blow in the blue air

We dance, we sing, we hope, we cheer.

Lilies and Asters grow in my heart

A chance of love in my life at last.

For next few months, I rejoice

While the nature swings, trees are moist.

I spin like a peacock in rain

Ezekiel and Akira through all pain.

He wipes my tears on days. dark

While I fear the future path.

I should have known it was too good to be true

I was born to die and rot and end in misery.

I should never have dragged them with me

Hindsight is such a cruel and vicious beast.

Now they will have to suffer my agony.

My past has now caught up with me.

Asher proposed to Naia, finally

We planned a party and went to the city.

"Naia, I don't think I can come with you."

"But... Aza, you are my only friend true."

She looked so lonely and betrayed and hurt

That I agreed without thinking of being alert.

Ezekiel knew I was hiding something

He asked me what I was still concealing.

He told me that Naia had a dangerous ability.

That's why they were all forced to go and flee.

He asked about my past.

So, I promised to tell after party at last.

"I will tell you a few things

My real name is Akira Minh.

From royals, I am on the run

That's why I wanted to stay hidden."

He nodded and hugged me tightly

"I trust you Akira. Don't worry."

Tears of joy, down my cheeks,

We kissed passionately and deep.

Celebrating the union of our friends

"Just live, Akira. Forget about future ends."

"You are right, honey. Let's live and love."

We grin, while storms brew above.

The prophecy again comes into play.

While on petals and clouds of pink, we lay.

A shadow dragon from rival kingdom attacks

Fire burns everything down, as it wreaks havoc

People's screams sing a horrible waltz

Lives, shops, houses and wills are lost.

Hundreds of arrows shower it,

While it dissolves again, mocking.

Streets painted in red puddles,

Darkness rises and shudders.

Zayn, Asher and Ezekiel help the children.

While Naia is nowhere to be seen.

I spot her running towards the unhinged beast,

"What are you doing, Naia?", I scream.

She keeps up her mad sprint.

I step in her path, stopping and trying.

"I am sorry Akira; I didn't tell you before

But my ability is that of shadows.

Only I can truly try to save us all

Please step back, I love you all."

My eyes wide, I fall down in a heap

"Get up!" Nair tries to lift.

"I thought, I was the prophesied one."

"I don't know what you are saying Akira."

"It has to be me, I am the master of shadows

I have golden eyes, that's why I am on the run."

"I thought you were unblessed."

"I lied.", I said

We both stare at each other,

Stunned and at a loss for ever.

I grip her hands, my resolve shining like sun.

"We will finish that monster, together. Run."

We lunge over torn, dirty rubble.

Striding through the city in trouble.

Ezekiel screeches at us, "Come back."

We raise our pace, cutting no slack.

A last gaze, a desperate plea, a final nod.

Wide eyes, terrified face, a hopeless sob.

A giant stream of shadows emerges, lush

Majestic, it escapes them in a deadly rush.

Naia and Akira, both stumble down.

Caught and held by Asher and Zayn.

The five friends watch, as the dragon howls.

An ear-shattering explosion of horrified growls.

Our eyes gleam, like firecrackers at night.

The world watches as darkness overpowers light.

The beast vanishes in an unseen void.

The city seems silent, still and coiled.

The royal guards rush towards the two girls.

While the three men stand around in a circle.

"King Desmond wants to meet you

Come with us. We won't hurt you."

The royals welcome us to the castle

Everyone seems overwhelmed, in a hustle.

King Desmond thanks, acts and preens

As if forgetting all about my arrest dreams.

Afterwards, the city of 'Everglean'

Is again polished, and gleams.

The sky dazzles a brilliant blue.

Flowers glow in scintillating hues.

The nature is again vibrant with colors,

Rainbows spill in patterned splatters.

"I love you, Akira.

The conqueror of my dreams.

The master of all things serene.

You bloom in my life, like a million stars

With you, I am forever high, floating afar.

You are all I ever want, need, feel and see

Tell me Akira, will you marry me?"

Ezekiel is kneeling before me

He looks so adorable and sweet.

I kneel with him, softly kissing his hand

The waves crash, my feet tickle in sand.

"Yes. Forever and ever, until the darkness ends

I will love you Ezekiel, until the starlight bends."

A royal wedding rings bells.

People wish, thank and bless.

Me and Ezekiel close in a kiss,

While Naia, Asher and Zayn encircle us.

Winds alive with songs of the stars,

The message of love, we learn at last.

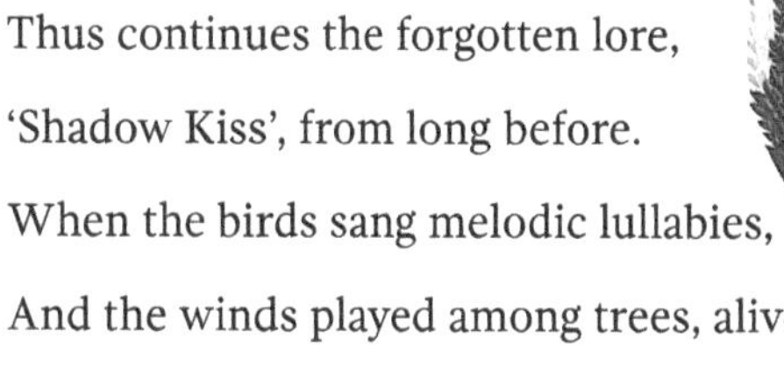

Thus continues the forgotten lore,

'Shadow Kiss', from long before.

When the birds sang melodic lullabies,

And the winds played among trees, alive.

When apples and sugar perfumed the air,

And the nature danced in a careless flair.

August and Autumn

White walls, sanitized scents
Intravenous drips and syringes.
The air reeks of desperation,
Sickness overpowers elation.
Mechanical whirrs of machines
Headache made me dizzy.

'Autumn Quinn' lay in her bed, groaning
Head throbbing and bones screaming.
A fractured arm, a cracked head
Splintered reality painted in red.
"How did I get here?
Oh yes, I remember."

She scowled at her blue robe,
Every part of her body throbbed.
She cursed the one who pushed and threw.
Her colorful vocabulary turned the air blue.
She felt a gaze on her, and turned,
Saw a man with a half-smile there.

She blushed at her unfiltered tirade.

Cheeks flaming at being heard.

"Looks like someone is mighty angry.

Those marshmallow earrings are quite fancy."

She touched her ears, checking them

"Yes, these fancy ones are very lucky."

Autumn breathed deep and took a look

His leg in a cast, hands carrying a book.

"No one is here with you?"

"Looks like you are alone too."

"I am, my parents disowned me."

"Is your injury, because of that?"

She shook her head, not wanting to tell

He offered a hand, "I am August Wells."

"Autumn Quinn, and I love the fall

Crisp air, apples, hot cocoa, and corn."

"Hmm. Looks like we are the same,

Autumn and August, isn't that lame?"

She smiled, a first in many days

Intrigued at his odd ways.

A girl arrived in a cloud of perfume and pink

She hugged Autumn and said, "You stink."

Autumn pushed her away, laughing

"Thanks for the praise, miss charming."

"This is Daisy, my friend.", she told August

They shook hands, following introductions.

"So, how did this happen?" Daisy asked both

August declared, "Don't laugh, I will go first."

"I got drunk with my friends last night

Fell and broke my leg due to blurry sight."

Both the girls snorted, while he glared

"I fell down the stairs." Autumn said.

Daisy's eyes narrowed at her lie.

Both knew that wasn't how or why

"Ha. At least I had a reason, Auti"

"Did you just call me 'Auti'?"

Colorful banter filled the canvas of air,

Tinkling euphoria and bubbles of care.

Washed out ambience comes alive,

Heartaches dull as passions arise.

"Where are your friends, by the way?"

"All lying face down on the floor, I say."

Both discharged from the hospital

Health stable and injury not fatal.

Leaves rain in a golden cascade

As silver sheets of winter fade.

Whispers of change in ember glow

The sky blushes, as relations weave slow.

Cole, Nick and Daisy, their friends

Weave together a tale without ends.

A blossom of delicacies in autumn,

Summer dissolves into fragrant cotton.

Chuckles, frowns, gasps and guffaws

Savory, sage, carnations and ferns.

August and Autumn bloom together

In a grandeur of camellias and asters.

Scented plumes of love adorn the winds

They work through their anxiety and whims.

Connection blazes as spices and sizzles

Jubilant as confetti, like chocolate drizzle.

"I hope I have gained enough trust now

To know about your injury and how?"

August asked her, one fine day in sun

He braced himself as Autumn began.

"Of course love, I trust you deep and whole

But I warn you, the past isn't all glam and rose."

A long inhale, eyes closed to bear the strain

Hands hold each other tight through the pain.

"I was offered a great opportunity

For my talent in math and skill.

Despite threats, I wanted to study better

So I packed, meaning to defy my father."

A faraway look in her moist eyes

Remembering the heart-wrecking ties.

"But my plans were irrelevant

Everything was engraved in sand.

His rage was as red as blood

Thick and sour like curdled milk."

Autumn's face was wet with tears shed

August hugged her as she softly whispered.

"He pushed me down the stairs

And that still gives me nightmares.

I fell down hard, bruised and broken

Hurt beyond words, sobbing and shaken."

Wrapping Autumn in his embrace

August said again and again.

"It's okay. I am here. Always.

Forever. Till the end of days.

I admire your resilience and courage, Auti

The bravest person I've met, you hear me?"

Months pass in a celestial waltz,

Stars stream by with radiant calls.

Planets spin in mindless pleasure,

The sun glitters with pride and leisure.

Meteors shower in staged symphonies,

Love wanders amid the vortex of galaxies.

"Autumn, you make me wish to shed all

All that is rotten, destined to fall.

I hope, I love, I live, I care, I dare

Just because you are with me, here.

Forevermore, I'll work to be worthy

But still I ask, will you marry me?"

Chants of "Yes!", glow bright as the ocean.

As August finally proposed Autumn.

He spins her in his arms as she shrieks

The couple kiss, amid bubbles of bliss.

A tale that began in dull white,

Now cloaked in rainbow delight.

But plans made are irrelevant

Everything is engraved in sand.

That day was dull, darp and gray

As if it were readying to prepare.

City dotted in clouds of gloom.

Rain in Autumn, predicts doom.

Both left, for a last date together

Before they became partners forever.

To talk and laugh about their first meet,

To wander through life's twisted streets,

To tear and erase past pains and sorrows,

To make a toast to dazzling tomorrows.

Belting off-tune tracks, while driving

They went for their bachelor party.

A huge truck moved towards them

Scared, they clutched each other's hands.

Horrible screeches of tires, panicked screams

A car accident and deadly agony flames.

Loud thunder cracked the surroundings

Sky shattered by fierce lightening.

Puddles of red on the rough road,

Tang of copper in the air soaked.

Sirens blare and scream an ear shattering howl.

Life bleeds as their hands touch one last hold.

Last smiles while gazing at their beloved,

Hearts fall still, in a semblance sacred.

Maybe it was a cruel accident.

Maybe staged by her parent.

Maybe their destiny, hopeless.

Maybe a term to justify helplessness.

Leaves still rain in a golden cascade,

As silver sheets of winter again fade.

Whispers of change in ember glow,

People die, some grieve, but lives flow.

And in the month of August

Autumn arrives in full swagger.

In the air, the trees still sway,

Shedding their past away.

As people come and go, on repeat

Crushing leaves beneath their feet.

Who remembers anyone in life's survival game?

Who remembers August and Autumn, so lame?

Flames and Friendship

Raven hair floating in phantom wind of night,

Eyes burning like twin golden flames in the dark.

Lips painted in the most gentle rose,

I narrate a tale, centuries old.

These two lands, eons old

At the dawn of time, when the world

Was shrouded in white, dense fog,

With everything sharp and cold.

There were two silver flame spirits

Sisters, named Eldor and Celeste.

They lived together on one realm,

But fate certainly had other plans.

A glittering violet spirit arrived,

Welcomed by the silvers, so naive.

Charming both sisters in a sinister game,

He wanted to break their kingdom's fame.

Both the spirits fell in love with violet

Insanely jealous, they became rivals.

A battle issued, rendering alive only a few

They cleaved their bird shaped land into two.

Their realm initially shaped

Like a bird with open wings.

Now the wings were cut off in a fit of rage.

Lands adrift, on distant shores, unclaimed.

Forever ashamed at their poison envy

The spirits bled and pleaded for mercy.

One last gift they left to the world

Before vanishing with the mist cold.

Their silver flames now blessed

Magic to the ones full of love and bliss.

Once again the realms unfurled

As Eldoria and Celestria cheered.

This was the tale of two kingdoms

Spanning colored vices and morals.

Now, let's hear the tale of Ava and Arial

Will their story end in ruins or cheer?

Avalon Silvern, an orphan girl,

Dimmed eyes like beaded pearls.

Childhood spent in the decaying streets

Desperate lanes of sweltering "Eldoria" heat.

Master of fire and ice magic

Her life was rough and tragic.

A rarity to own the power of reverse double

Especially for a "scum from street rouble".

Arial Kane, a girl in her late teens
Admiring the dew kissed greens.
Hair as vibrant as the sun's rays
Gleaming aqua eyes, like ocean waves.

Known as the oceanic enchanter,
The waves and water spellcaster.
The princess of the lavish kingdom of Eldoria
A life spent in dazzling grandeur and euphoria.

Eldoria, a sprawling expanse of exquisite splendor
Adorned in gardenias, willows, basils and clover.
Majestic trees of alluring beauty
Dancing to a private melody.

Avalon, Arial's help and maid,
Princess's only friend and mate.
Fierce like wildlife, free and untamed.
Cold like ice, brutal and unrelenting.

"Ava, I ... wanted to talk to you"

"What is it? You look like wilted dew"

"I don't! I look like ... sweet candy", Arial glared

"More like a sour and sticky one", Ava murmured.

"Ugh! You know, prince Connor is courting me."

"Who? That ape boy with heart like a rotten pea"

"Exactly, rumors say he is worse than the devil!"

"For your sake, I hope they are untrue, Arial."

"He is arriving today."

"Your only choice is to pray"

Arial laughed at last, amid creeping shadows

And Ava smiled, even as her heart thundered.

Prince Connor Gold of Celestria

Shrouded in mists of mysteria.

Confident and calm, named the skydancer

Owing to his brilliant magic of thunder.

People fear the unknown

Connor is just a clone.

Bounded by the ghost of forlornness,

He wanders in the streets of loneliness.

Celestria, a glowing realm of radiant yellow

Honeysuckle, sunflower and citrus rose.

Melting gold fields of wheat and mustard

Perfumed air alive with the song of birds.

Goldspun Celestria enters the Emerald Eldoria

Arial fears the future, on the verge of hysteria.

"Rumors are like feathers, mate

It's rare that either holds weight"

"You are just saying to calm me"

"I ... uh, is it working?"

Arial groaned dramatically

Ava cackled loud and heartily.

They all entered the warm living room
Adorned in wreaths of wisteria bloom.
The interior was simple yet intricate
Painted vases, elegant teapot and plate.

King Ivander Kane seated on his ornate chair
Connor at his side, dressed with elegant care.
Tousled blond tresses caressed his nape,
The handsome male was far from an ape.

Arial was dressed in a blush cloudy dress
Delicate embroidery and careful frills.
Ava standing with her head bowed,
Quietly ushering the servant crowd.

"I welcome you to Eldoria, Prince Connor
This is Princess Arial, my lovely daughter."
King Ivander, acting so welcoming and serene!
Why is Arial to him, so unmerited and unseen?

A soft smile, "Good Evening, prince"

"Just Connor please", he winced

"Of course Connor, how do you fare today?

I hope you are enjoying your stay"

"I am quite splendid, thank you

Eldoria rejuvenates me anew.

So, how are you coping at seeing me?

I know the rumors claim me terrifying"

Aria startled at the prince's cavalier inquiry

"I admit, you are ... unexpected, truly"

Connor laughed, deep and husky

"A wise choice of words indeed."

Words flowing like silk sheets

Glittering bubbles of letters adrift.

Chuckles, gasps and twinkling eyes

Ember alight as a connection arise.

"How would you describe the ocean wide?"

Connor blinked, surprised "I personify it as life"

"As the ocean doesn't exist without waves grace

Life isn't worth living without challenges grave."

Arial was pleasantly surprised and awed

Ava could see proverbial hearts around her.

And as the obsidian night drew closer

She feared the motives of King Ivander.

"It was a treat meeting you princess wise."

Arial blushed, and glowed like sea at sunrise.

"You too aren't that terrifying"

The royals departed smiling.

Arial was floating on peonies and rose.

The sky was raining crimson confetti hoards.

"Don't be too happy yet, dear

Fierce rains often succeed early cheer"

Ava was contented to see

Her friend soo jubilant and free.

Arial deserved all the goodness.

The girls hugged in a hearty caress.

The day of wedding was decided.

The nuptials would be solemnized

Four months from today,

In a plum pink and ochre affair.

Arial and Connor often went on luncheons

Ava as a chaperone, accompanied them on.

Scintillating dazzles of daisy love.

Dandelion floats in the air above.

Preparations for the grand union

Joyous beats and succulent violin.

A celestial symphony of elation calls

Asters and winds play a fairy tale waltz.

Months flow fluid like Arial's water
Marked with Connor's enigmatic thunder.
While Ava lit blazing stars in their lives,
Even as she feared future hails of ice.

Spring arrived in scented plumes of tinkling blooms
Sky awashed in pails of ethereal cosmic hues.
Butterflies dancing and squirrels singing
The merry nature was celebrating.

Arial looked heavenly in a fantasy gown.
Her hairs adorned with a snowflake crown.
Gossamer velvet clipped with pearls blue.
A trail of water, weaving forth, playing lute.

Prince Connor stood tall and regal, at the altar.
A deep indigo cloak cascaded down his shoulders.
Edges laced with frost of thunder, bright.
Amethyst gems glinting in the sunlight.

His silver eyes soft and full of love

Awaiting Arial, his life's joyful dove.

She arrived as an angel of infinitesimal beauty

Both hearts running unhinged, beating crazily.

The priest delivers the solemn sermons.

Aqua and silver eyes lock like triggered guns.

"And over all these virtues put on love,

which binds them all together in perfect unity."

"In presence of nature and my family dear

I claim you mine and give up all fear.

I vow to protect you in times dark

From your love, I would never shirk"

"On days somber, I will be by your side

On days bright, we will both rejoice.

I vow to cherish you with all my might

On gloomy dawns and obsidian nights"

"Together we'll build a life of trust and care,

Facing the world as a united pair.

In sickness and health, till the end of our days,

With these vows, our love forever stays."

As Arial moved to kiss her husband

A shot sounded, fracturing and sudden.

A broken cry, scarlet stains on white

King Ivander did act his horrible blight.

Ava fell down in a broken heap,

Her heart gushing blood like crazy.

She gasped, a wretched wet wail,

Her eyelids heavy, her skin pale.

The cold metal bullet

Did pierce the heart

Not of the intended, Connor

But innocent Ava's.

A horrible sound of grief came from Arial

She kneeled at her friend's selfless feet.

King Ivander soon surrounded by soldiers

But Arial's heart was already in cinders.

"Why did you come in the way Ava?"

"Arial, I always want your pleasure"

"What will I do without you?"

"I believe... Connor... will take care of you"

"Please don't leave me alone,

You are the only one"

"Oh dear, I wish you ... Love

You were ... my ... only friend..."

Arial cried as her friend died.

Connor hugged her tight.

Ivander wanted to rule Celestria

But Ava's courage, gifted a utopia.

The wind howls in wretched wails tonight

A haunting melody, eerie in the onyx quiet.

Ashen eyes, damp and veined with red

Stare at the cracked ceiling overhead.

Tap, tap, tap

Heart screaming to flee

Her spine crawling

with phantom feels.

Time doesn't heal the wounds

Just covers them, as we rue.

Years pass, in an agonizing crawl.

Connor helps Arial throughout it all.

In the end, they just thank the stars and the wind

For gifting them a life

Of glorious passion and grins.

Connor and Arial rule both the kingdoms

As silver and azure linings blossom.

A fine radiant day, a child is born.

In spring, at the break of dawn.

Cloaked in flames of starlight,

Arial cradles her cherubic child.

A girl endowed to the enchanted rulers,

Wrapped in a halo of moonbeam sparkles.

Connor kissed her soft sweet hands

Naming the babe, Avalon Kane.

Winds whispered through the trees

As the parents beamed in blessed bliss.

Remembering their daring old friend,

Who is forever alive as hope godsend.

And as the sun sets on Eldoria's land,

And Celestria's golden fields expand,

Together, they unravel the secrets untold

Writing a new chapter, in the legends of old.

For in the realm

Where raven hair dances

On phantom wind,

And eyes gleam

With the fire of twin golden flames.

Lips adorned

In the softest hues of rose,

A new chapter begins,

As their story unfolds.

Crystal Tears

Crystal teardrop strings, delicate and cold

Suspend from sorrowed eyes.

Heartbreaking promises

And devastating lies.

Red streaks the misty depths of despair

A fragile haze of hope looms ahead.

Entangled in pale, aching strands of pain

The vibrant hues of life drained like rain.

Wounds bestowed by my dearest.

Veiled commands, blindly issued.

Pierce the worst.

Shatter my worth.

Call me emotionally barren?

As you say my tears are inert!

How dare you diminish my worth?

When you call my emotions mere manipulative gears!

I hide them now,

Naming them pretty jewels.

See how my eyes gleam in the sun!

Adornments hanging like abominations.

You lost the right to kiss them,

When you made me taste the saltiness.

The windows to my souls,

To you, are forever closed.

I wait, hoping

That one day, someone

Will cherish my tears

Hold them close,

Claim them as theirs.

Broken Petals

The birds sing a gentle melody.

Trees sway in sacred symphonies.

The sky blushes like a fresh rose.

Winds whistle the nature prose.

Fairy lights adorn the lush garden

Asters and lavender, Daisies and fern.

The wedding ceremony is vibrant

Pink bubbles of happiness, radiant.

I smile and glow in a gossamer gown

Wreath of azalea, on my head as a crown.

I go down the aisle, beside my father

Gazing at 'Parker', my life, my lover.

'Azalea' he says my name in a reverent whisper

I turn to mush, as my heart flutters.

We gaze deep into each other's eyes.

The priest recites sermons of eternal ties.

"I do." forever binds us in our holy vows

We kiss, we dance, we cheer and hope.

We live together floating on magical sand

I think about how lucky I am.

But appearances are often fake

My decisions might be a result of haste.

People hide behind numerous masks

What did I do? The future me would ask.

It began slowly, almost a crawl,

Crafty insults to make me feel small.

It began to run, in a couple years,

Temper tantrums and shattering wares.

And then it grew wings, soaring high,

A slap, a push, a fracture, a lie.

"No! Don't hurt me, please."

"Apologize, get down on your knees."

Broken screams sing a horrible waltz

Tears mix with blood as all will is lost.

Abuse is bleak, emotions leak.

A ray of sun, my blurry eyes seek.

Azalea no longer signifies joy and romance

My Wails mix with the agony of violence.

"You are mine. You do what I say.

I am your God. You work my way."

His awful words burn like acid

I see his face, rotten and rancid.

"You won't ever own me, Parker

I will make you sorry, remember."

I am a bird, with cut off wings

I am a fish, dying out of the sea.

I am mocked and locked.

My heart pains in brutal throbs.

But I won't let that monster win

He deserves to pay for his sins.

And if I have to become a devil for that,

I would gladly take my revenge, blood in hands.

So, I hear but don't listen.

I plot as my tears glisten.

Careful traps, intense stealth

Purchase of poisons promising death.

Silence in motion, duplicity in acts

I face humiliations with all I have.

Nothing would hinder my plans.

I would make sure of that.

One gloomy Sunday, the wind howls

As if mourning my break of holy vows.

I slip a poison in the dinner

Time to finish off that damn sinner!

I sit near his feet, as instructed

Head bowed, legs tucked, submissive.

I wait for him to eat the cake

But he gets up and goes back.

"Won't you eat the dessert?"

"I won't. Your cake tastes like dirt."

"I promise. I made it better today."

"Why are you so insistent, by the way?"

I grit my teeth, "You love cheesecake."

"Yeah, but you seem suspicious and fake."

He prowls towards me, intimidating

I refuse to back down, standing.

He obviously suspects her.

Will I ever get rid of this monster?

"I am surprised it took you this long.

I know you are quite mentally strong."

And just when he reaches for my throat

I impale him with a knife, hidden in dress folds.

Drops of red splatter my face

I am sure, I look like a savage.

His eyes were wide in betrayal and rage

As if he is the most innocent sage.

I twist the knife deeper into his gut,

Watching blood flow in scarlet rivers.

His wretched choking fills the air

I close my eyes, soaking up his fear.

He falls down, I go with him
I stab him again and again.
My wrath and vengeance at last,
This moment so tranquil yet fast.
A hush fills the house.
The air feels hollow.

This moment of quiet
So peaceful and right.
I bask in its precious light.
"God bless you.", they say.
"Too late.", I lament.
"The devil already did."

A sudden beeping fills my ears,
My heart gallops as my head clears.
My sight blurs as Parker vanishes
A strange white noise emerges.
Whispers of beings in the air
Sanitized scents sterile and bare.

My eyelids feel heavy, sealed

My limbs are frozen, I can't feel.

And as my eyes open and adjust

I know that I am in a hospital.

It was all a dream;

I couldn't kill him.

Parker sits beside my stretcher

He looks concerned, the liar.

He sees me awake, and turns pale

He knows his abuse will be unveiled.

A man comes, old and somber.

"I am glad to see you awake Mrs. Ember.

Do you know how you got here?"

"I do" my weak voice whispers.

"Well, you fell down the stairs

Your husband brought you here.

You were in coma for three weeks

Parker never left. You are so lucky.

I will give you two time to talk.

I have taken blood tests, let's await the results."

I wanted to stop him,

But my tongue felt heavy.

Parker already tried to kill me once

I am sure this time he will succeed.

I failed miserably during that dinner

I wish it happened like in my slumber.

Parker leans over me, his gaze cold.

This narcissistic and cruel jerk!

"I can't let you live dear.

My life, my career, I fear."

He closes my eyes with his palm, like a lover.

I try to speak through the oxygen mask, in fear.

"You should have never gone against me.

Now, you would have to die, you see."

He frowns as if there was no way.

I want to scratch his eyes off his face!

"I won't tell." I mumble shakily

My last try, my last futility.

He shakes his head sadly, mocking,

And steps on my oxygen tube

Tears fill my eyes,

He feels so huge.

I can't breathe. I choke.

I flutter like a dead bird, alone.

My gasps paint the air blue

I struggle, but it's no use.

My life force bleeds,

And no one rues.

I eventually lose myself

Drowning in tides of grief and hate.

I float above, gazing down at the broken girl

She looks so young, so fragile, so small.

I look at the man standing near

He dusts his hand, as if to clear.

His eyes are empty as ever.

He sits down, without any care.

I died while dreaming of lies

I hoped while I lay dying

I wept while I kept hoping

I suffered while I was weeping.

I trembled while I suffered in tears.

I did nothing while I trembled with fear.

Now I float and fly

Up and up, to kiss the sky.

Azalea left behind far and below.

I tumble with the winds of mellow.

I flutter in red gardens of lushness.

I live the happiness, I never expected.

Some monsters live

And some innocents die.

I wander the houses that are settled,

Wondering about Azalea's broken petals.

As the sky blushes like a fresh rose

And winds whistle the nature prose.

Shades of Life

~~ Scene 1 ~~

My hands glide and

Paints whisper.

Calm blue hues,

Serene whites on paper.

The sky is infinite,

My sheet's just a square.

It seems unfair,

Capturing it here.

It seems wrong,

Limiting the limitless.

Children laugh near me.

Tagging through the park lanes.

Their cheeks are red.

Hair a shade darker

Due to heat and sweat.

Eyes, jagged crystals

Like broken stars,

Flaming at night.

I smile.

Continue to paint the sky.

I am shading the edges,

When I feel a soft tap

on my shoulder.

I turn to see,

And immediately

Freeze.

A girl stands behind me,

Her eyes, a vortex of galaxies.

Blue, pink, purple, red

Whirlpool of melting palette,

Swirling as if

Dancing in space.

Someone clears their throat,

Loudly.

The girl raises a single eyebrow.

I blink.

Her pupils turn black.

I blink again.

Black dissolves into brown.

"Are you a moron?"

Her question

Knocks on my mind.

I refocus.

Ignore the ever-changing eyes,

It must be a trick of light.

"It's rude to bully people."

I tell her.

She rolls her now-green eyes.

Sighs and sits beside me

On the bench.

Her hair, black.

Like midnight rain puddles.

White sweatshirt

Colorful jeans.

Odd.

"I didn't bully you.

I asked you respectfully."

My eyes narrow.

Is she teasing me?

Is she lying?

Or is she herself a moron?

Yes, last one makes sense.

"I am not a moron.

But, why did you ask?"

She points at my painting,

"Due to that bland

Monstrosity of yours."

She says casually, shrugging.

My eyes widen in outrage.

How dare she!

"Oh! And you think

You could do better?"

I challenge.

Raise my eyebrows,

Mimicking her.

She rolls her purple eyes again.

"I'd have to do sky-searching first."

She says as if it's obvious.

I grind my teeth.

"And what's that supposed to mean?"

I ask the arrogant know-it-all.

She looks at me.

I look back.

And count

One

Two

Three

... Sixty-one.

"We have to search the perfect sky."

She nods towards my sheet

"So that you can paint better."

"And why would I do that?"
She shrugs again,
"I don't paint.
I direct."
I stare at her,
Exasperated
Yet intrigued.
"And then?"
I ask.

She looks deep into my eyes,
Cherry red against my baby blue.
"Wait, Watch, Warn, and then
Warrant."
My breath stutters.
I shift back, uncomfortable.

She is still waiting for my answer.
I take a deep breath
Hoping this is the right decision
And say, "So, when do we leave
For sky searching?"

"Past is lost,

Future is away.

Let's leave now,

What do you say?"

Her eyes glitter golden.

How can I deny the dare?

~~ Scene 2 ~~

"So, what's your name?"

I ask my mystery companion.

She is sitting on the passenger seat.

Her oil-black hair

Fluttering in the wind,

As my car speeds through the lanes.

She turns to me,

Emeralds in her eyes,

"Names are nothing.

Just lost letters in wind.

Fireflies in the sun

Only meant to burn"

The wheels skid

Dangerously.

I maneuver the car.

Get back to driving.

I see her on the

Periphery of my vision.

She is sitting still.

I try to collect my thoughts.

But they are adrift,

Lost in the storm

Of this alluring labyrinth.

"How about I give you a name?"

I ask, my voice clear.

I swallow and wait.

I don't want to force her.

I want to be her friend.

Maybe she didn't like her name?

"What name do you have in mind?"

She says at last.

I squeal internally.

Patting myself for the win.

Externally, I act relaxed.

She is like a pretty illusion,

A fantasy, I can't touch.

So...

"What about Mirage?"

She doesn't respond.

Then says quietly.

"I like it."

I am about to utter a cheer,

When,

"But isn't it kind of long?"

I deflate.

"How about a short version?

Mira for Mirage."

She smiles.

I stare.

Then face ahead.

Drive.

Should I reveal my name?

I don't know.

Let's just do it.

I clear my throat.

"I am Iris."

Hold my breath,

Wait.

"Hmm. Rainbow.

Colorful name!"

"Thanks."

We share a smile.

Laugh.

Go on

~~ Scene 3 ~~

"What about this sky?"

I ask Mira.

She shakes her head.

I squint at the noon sun.

White light blinds me.

I look down

Colors twirl in my vision.

Fragmented circles

In rainbow clusters.

"Why? I think it's fine."

I ask, irritated.

She sighs.

"It's dull. Smooth.

No upheavals.

A plain plane.

Purity can't be absolute.

Vibrance can't be relative."

I stay silent.

Because I know she is right.

She crosses her arms,

"How can you choose?

When you haven't seen it all.

How can you decide?

When you haven't felt it all."

She looks at me.

Her silver eyes

Like metal.

Sharp and deadly.

"Now, what do you want?

Fine?

Or divine?"

Mirage is wise;

Her voice, a hypnotic dream.

Her rhetorical question

Is enough

To change me.

Who knew illusions could be philosophical?

I purse my lips,

Nod,

Change the gear,

Drive ahead.

~~ Scene 4 ~~

"Look at the fields!

Now, that's divine."

My car is parked

on the muddy path.

Dust plumes float like flames.

Particles glow in light.

To the right,

Paddy fields

Shimmer velvet green.

To the left,

Mustard melts

Like golden butter.

Mira rolls her yellow eyes.

Her arms fold.

Feet tapping on the ground.

"Iris, your perception of divine

Is ridiculous."

I huff.

Fold my arms.

Look away.

She always shuts me up.

Mira isn't thoughtful

At all.

"Okay. That was rude.

I will say it again.

And try to explain."

Mira sounds apologetic,

Her eyes are silver and soft.

I stare,

Entranced.

Give a nod,

A chance.

She begins.

"Yellow and green

Are wealth unclaimed,

Unseen.

Purity is the seed,

While growth is the root.

Renewal is the strength

That kisses it anew."

My eyebrows scrunch

In confusion.

"Then why?"

I shake my head.

She loves to speak

In riddles.

She holds my hand.

Her grip is soft and warm.

"Tell me Iris

Do you crave the seed,

Or the fruit?

Do you admire the leaf,

Or the root?

Is it sweetness you seek

Or the bitter shoot?"

She pauses.

Giving me time

To contemplate.

Then,

"Is it the relative serenity you want

Or the divinity of absolute?"

She steps near me,

Her eyes, a spiral of yellow and green.

Her voice, a hot whisper

In the cold air.

I shiver,

And it's not due to cold.

"Do you fear the halves,

Or do you fear the complete?

Tell me Iris, what do you feel?"

My lips part,

Eyes widen.

My mind sizzles.

Her voice plays in my head

On repeat.

And decide,

I might want halves,

But I need completes.

I blink.

She is standing away from me.

I take a deep breath,

Roll up my sleeves,

Open the car door,

And call her to have a seat.

We have miles to go

Before we sleep.

~~ **Scene 5** ~~

Ominous gray clouds

Drape the sky.

Scent of water

Hangs in the air.

"We have come far from the city.

It's about to rain, shortly."

I tell Mira.

Worried, that she might leave.

Mira says nothing.

Just sits in the car's backseat.

"Um... Mira? ...

Mirage?"

She pats the space beside her.

I frown,

But sit.

Her golden skin,

Dazzles amid the grays.

"Why didn't you consider

Painting this sky?"

She asks,

Her voice loud

Over the sound of thunder.

She looks at me,

Her gray eyes, ringed in blue.

"Why didn't you think

This sky deserved a painting?"

I open my mouth.

Close it.

I try to form words,

But they slip like vapors in wind.

My throat rattles,

But silence is vast.

My tongue flutters,

But the sounds are lost.

My sanity is trapped

Within the web of my thoughts.

"I... It's dark."

I offer lamely.

The silence ahead

Feels oppressive.

A burden

Sitting on my back.

Why didn't I draw?

I don't know.

Or maybe ... I do?

Mira stares at me,

Without blinking.

Eerie.

Intense.

Still.

Behind her,

The windows glow white

In streaks of light.

"There are just black and gray

No colours at play.

The dim skies wail

In a melancholy affair.

I don't want to paint,

Because I feel fear."

I say, my voice small.

Head down,

Feeling pretty

And vulnerable.

Mirage shakes her head.

Her hair

Now a mess of wild curls.

She faces ahead,

Leans her head on my shoulder,

Her arms around her waist.

Voice velvet as sin,

"Dark is the mud

In which seeds we sow.

Dark is the soil

In which cotton fields grow.

Dark is the night

In which the silver stars glow.

Dark is the valley

Through which the amethyst rivers flow.

Dark is the universe

Whose magnificence is widely known."

My eyes are wide,

But her's shut close.

Words barely audible

But still loud in my ears,

"Dark are the windows

Carrying raindrops and tears along.

Dark are the long lanes

Where we love to wander alone.

Dark are the hearts

That reflect our soul.

Dark are our minds

When it's us, we try to fool."

I gasp.

Lightning blinds the sky,

The car windows glow

In rain.

I close my eyes,

Cover my ears.

Open up,

And see black hole eyes

Inches from my face.

Thunder shrieks.

Rain competes.

Mira continues,

Mercilessly.

"Now try and dare

To downplay the dark.

I know, it's cold and rough

Enough to leave marks."

She leans her forehead

Against mine.

I allow.

"But it's cool and familiar too,

Like an old friend so true.

Burnt browns and ashen grays,

Tricky and mischievous

But still our solace."

My hands shake.

I trap them,

Inside my unrolled sleeves.

Mira again leans her head

Against my side.

I bite my lower lip,

Deep and hard.

Lick the blood,

And enjoy the dark.

~~ Scene 6 ~~

"What is your opinion, Ms. Mirage?

Is this sky perfect for our art?"

I ask my lovely Mirage.

She rolls her pink eyes again.

I wonder how

they haven't stuck in the back yet.

Sure, I know they are ... interesting,

Doesn't mean they need to keep rolling.

"What is your view first?"

She asks curiously.

Her eyes,

Wide and trusting.

I look around.

The valley is lush,

Its tip, unseen.

Mist-filled skies,

Touched with green.

Treacherous gray paths,

Their beauty unknown.

To kiss the pearl white fog,

The crimson sun sinks alone.

Dusk comes close,

Land runs infinite.

Awash in red gold,

Wet grass twirls in delight.

Twisted lanes,

In and deep.

Black shadows linger,

Behind the trees.

My boots are heavy,

The flowers stalk.

They trail behind,

Echoing my walk.

Purple and pink,

Oranges in deep ink.

The sky blushes like a bride

Adorned in rainbow half-rings.

I look at her,

Smile, showing teeth

"Divine."

She tips her head back,

Laughs.

Like chimes in night rain.

"Yes Iris

All shades together

Always make life better."

She winks.

I blink.

Mira continues,

"Life is most beautiful

When we embrace

All its colours.

Nature is the tapestry

Of life.

And it's colours

Make it divine."

I nod my head.

Thinking.

Dreaming.

I sit under a tree.

Its shade,

A cloak of safety.

Mira sits beside me,

Her eyes,

Scintillating cascades

Of eternal change.

We talk about

Nothing

And everything.

Paint the sky

During the silences

In between.

At last, It's the end

Of our sky-searching.

As the rain subsides

To a drizzle,

Colours turn murkier,

And darkness creeps

On toes,

The painting

Is complete.

The canvas is a blend

Of ethereal hues.

Red passion

Igniting

In flames of

Yellow sunshine

And orange bliss.

Purple silent in its wisdom,

Pink sprinkling

Love kisses.

Blue whispering calm

To the renewing green.

White, a dash of purity

To the mystery of

Black seas.

Gray and silver,

Strands of

Dazzling patience.

And gold,

The frame of success

And wellness.

I look at the sheet

In my hand.

Proud of myself,

And grateful for my friend.

I turn to Mira,

Give her a hug.

She stands frozen and stiff

But eventually

Hugs me back.

I smile at her,

She smiles back.

"Iris, you are a great and kind girl.

I hope you have a life

As colourful

As your name.

Now, I must leave

So that we can meet again and again."

She gets up to go

I hold her hand.

"Please stay."

I plead.

She holds my cheek

I lean into her hand.

"Live and love

Every shade of life, Iris.

We will meet again,

I promise."

Her hand leaves my skin.

I immediately miss

The warmth of it.

She walks,

I call her,

"Mirage!"

She halts.

Doesn't turn.

"Tell me your name, at least.

Please!"

She tilts her head to the side,

Only her eyes are visible,

A swirling mix

Of coloured crystals.

"Life."

She whispers,

Turns,

And walks into the abyss of darkness.

Or maybe, the freedom of blankness.

Long after Life leaves,

I stand

Beneath the obsidian sky,

The stars like pearls on

The fabric of night.

I stand and I think,

I think about every moment,

 Every word again.

I think about Mirage.

No, Life again.

"I don't paint. I direct."

"Wait, watch, warn and then

Warrant."

I think and I wonder,

Is my life, a mirage?

Or,

Is my mirage, life?

I wonder and I sleep.

I sleep and I dream.

Colours in smoke,

Blowing all around me.

While I sit with

Mirage, my Life

And paint and paint

The sky on sheets.

Does It Hurt?

You were drowning in the emotion fight.

Clenching your twitching fingers tight.

Your nails bit into your soft palms,

Red blood flowed, cold and dark.

You were sobbing, alone and bereft

Does it hurt, knowing they left?

You sat or maybe hid in the washroom.

The air was thick with despair and gloom.

You covered your mouth with your hands

Wiping tears with the toilet paper napkins.

You tried to choke, like a fish in the air.

Does it hurt, knowing they didn't care?

Your face was wrecked in blotches red

You tasted salt in the wetness wretched.

The dew kissed green of your lovely eyes

Cowered behind the fiery crimson tides.

You inhaled deep, as your heart seared.

Does it hurt, knowing they laughed near?

The waterfalls of lament eventually fall bare

You breathe heavy lung-fulls of rancid air.

Loud gasps interrupt the hollow hush

Your legs shake with the sensation rush.

Your eyes barely open up now, dear.

Does it hurt, knowing they sang cheers?

You stand tall, erect, in a perfect posture.

Your perfect smile, glows with fake luster.

Your palms bleed, but the backside is perfect

Your eyes are perfect emeralds, in numb effect.

You come out of the washroom, tall and erect.

Does it hurt, knowing they were truly perfect?

Astrid

I knew we were doomed from the start.

Still I went ahead, not wanting to part.

Was I a coward for loving you?

Or selfish for keeping you?

Does love lie in letting you go?

Not fighting for an ever more?

You pushed, I pursued.

My silly heart, you misused.

You begged to let go,

I tightened my hold.

You said no, I craved more.

Even if it meant losing my core.

It would never work, they said.

How could I not even try, Astrid?

You lit my veins in a million stars

I was high on you, floating afar.

Your touch burned me in divine ways

Your words slept with me for days.

You were an incarnation of your namesake

A beautiful goddess to bless us peasants.

You loved me, you cared, you smiled at me

And I lit up like a child on Christmas morning.

I was lost in the haze of mindless euphoria

Astrid, you made me want to be better.

I cried, I tried and I failed

You were still uncertain and afraid.

I love you but we are impossible, you said

Your lack of trust, it broke me Astrid.

I made you mine through nights long

Only to watch you step back at dawn.

I was wretched, I screamed

Like a fish in air, I floundered.

I fluttered like a bird with broken wings

My heart lay fractured in sharp glass pieces.

I limped like an animal with torn limbs

Because I was limp without you, Astrid.

You left like you came, in a whirlwind

While I was left miserable and gasping.

My tears leak like smoke from fire

I am weeping, then fuming with cold ire.

Why couldn't you fight for us, Astrid?

Didn't I deserve even a little effort?

I have lost my mind, I am unhinged

Did you want to see me hurt, Astrid?

That is the problem with me

When I feel, I drown in it completely.

Your love, how I craved desperately!

Now I writhe in my own agony.

We can't force others to feel as deeply

That is the hard slap of cold reality.

You didn't even try to consider me

I longed for a chance of passion, truly.

Even if you chose to give up and flee, darling

I will keep swimming in our memories, smiling.

The Embrace

She glows like a diamond in rain

I admire her wide toothed grin.

Her eyes are wide and earnest

Her cherubic face, truly the best.

She kisses my cheek, laughing

I close my eyes, reminiscing.

Under July's sweltering blaze,

The sun gleamed as birds took flight in a haze.

I stood in a stifling room, perspiring,

Pacing back and forth, my heart tiring.

Spacious yet homey, the room stood,

The stretcher lay, an island misunderstood.

Fidgeting, I await my father's call,

Dreaming of our new joy's enthral.

I gaze at the walls, the sterile tiles,

Hoping the baby brightens our lives.

A tinkling ring shatters the thick hush,

I fumble with the phone in anxious rush.

"You have a baby sister now, dear,

'Didi' chants will soon fill the air."

I stand mute, words lost in a blur,

My heart races in a painful spur.

Tears spill, my face is wet,

Unsure why tears fall like that

Silent, my mom entered the room,

She lay on her bed, still as gloom.

A small babe was nestled in sheets

Cocooned in the blanket pleats.

Her eyes are closed, her lids flutter

Her sight leaves me to stutter.

"She is so ... small," I whisper,

I keep staring her way, in a quiver.

Her hands are like my doll's,

So soft, tiny, and pink as dawn.

Gazing at her thin lips,

I wipe my eyes, tears adrift.

I thank God for His blessing

I touch her rosy cheeks, caressing.

Her feet are the length of my pinky finger

Her hair is short like petals, tender.

She seems to be haloed in shimmering sunlight

For the first time, I believe in love at first sight.

My mother gazes at me, smiling

I grin back at her, my heart wildly dancing

"She is so little and delicate

A gift from stars and heavenly fate.

I will always protect her

I love her, mama, forever."

I giggle like a toddler myself,

I twirl in glitters of bliss and relief.

The sky seems covered in cotton candy,

The white walls gleam in gentle light,

I throw my head back and shout,

"I thank the divine for this dream bestowed."

I jolt back to now, as she tugs my hand,

"Come on, Didi," Keerat kicks up the sand.

"Coming, sugar," I follow her lead,

We sit together on the lively beach.

"Let's make a castle, please help me."

"You dig a tunnel; I'll fetch water from the sea."

We kneel to build, focused,

Together we create a lovely castle.

Our parents arrive, we preen,

Their eyes shine with a golden sheen.

Our papa twirls us in his safe arms,

While mama dusts our dirty palms.

Together we stand near the emerald sea,

My heart blooms like lilies in dazzling glee.

The sun rises like a bird, in radiant rays,

My family is close, like a warm embrace.

I clutch my sister's hand, tight and sure,

And vow to guard this happiness forever.

Believe Anew

I walk the dark roads, forlorn,

Bare, rough, and hard-worn.

I know what lies ahead,

Every detail carved in my head.

I still tread the despised lanes,

Soaking up the lusciousness of sins.

Like an addict lost in a maze,

I wander the haze in a daze.

Many figures share this laze of indulgence

Each lost in bliss and then repentance.

I am not alone, but lonely

Coldness of shadows drowns me, slowly.

I know the walk of shame.

Craving the taste of the depraved

My feet don't stop,

My sanity is robbed.

Footprints no longer in sand, but in stone

Oh! How I wish and long to atone.

I want to turn back

My spine is stiff, my movements slack.

I hunch and crawl.

The winds seem to howl.

Marks etched here forever

Yet redemption dances mindlessly near.

I stumble where splendid splendor lies

The sudden bright hurts my eyes.

But the warmth can't be stolen

And for one terrifying moment, I hope to believe.

I wandered the wailing lands

And tasted hatred on my hands.

Monsters lurk in temptation's corridor

Becoming part of my memory's lore.

Hard to let go, the vines of the wicked.

They won't grab me; I won't be led.

I am naked to the stars

Now, I won't be behind golden bars.

My heart is fickle and wretched

Like crystal balanced on a knife's edge.

I will save this life-gifting scarred tissue

Even if it's shriveled, I will gift it true

Breathing in, pure life anew...

The End

Acknowledgments

First and foremost, without the hands of divine guiding me at all times, this book would not have been possible. I thank Waheguru for blessing me with the gift of words and imagination.

To my father, Bhupinder Singh, thank you for your unwavering love and support. Your belief in me has been the cornerstone of my journey. You are my life light.

To my mother, Sandhya, thank you for being my biggest fan and critic. Your tough love keeps me going.

To my sister, Upkeerat, who never fails to make me laugh when I'm stressed, thank you for always being there to brighten my days. Your laughter is the music that keeps my spirit light.

To my grandparents, thank you for never losing faith in me. Your wise presence and steadfast belief continue to inspire me.

To my best friend, Prisha Rana, thank you for always hyping me up and reminding me of my potential. You believed in me when no one else did. You encouraged me when I was down. You are and will always be my ride or die. Love you dude.

A heartfelt thank you to my publication manager, Rendha Fasil and the whole team at Notion press for your invaluable guidance and for believing in my vision. You helped me to shape my dream into reality.

I am deeply grateful to my teachers who saw potential in me and encouraged me to pursue my passion for writing.

A special thank you to my friends and relatives who have supported me throughout this journey. Your love and encouragement have been invaluable.

Finally, to my readers, thank you from the bottom of my heart. Your support and love for 'Eternal Whispers: Songs of the Soul' mean the world to me. This book is for you. May these poems resonate with you and bring a touch of magic to your lives. Thank you for allowing me to share my heart and soul with you.